INSIDE THE BOX

 FriesenPress

One Printers Way
Altona, MB R0G 0B0
Canada

www.friesenpress.com

ISBN
978-1-03-833056-7 (Hardcover)
978-1-03-833055-0 (Paperback)
978-1-03-833057-4 (eBook)

1. COMPUTERS, ENTERPRISE APPLICATIONS

Distributed to the trade by The Ingram Book Company

INSIDE THE BOX

Mastering Internal Product Management

ILANA J. SPRONGL

Contents

Foreword

The book you are holding in your hand—or viewing on your screen—is unique because it ventures into an often-overlooked corner of product management: the world of internal products. In a field dominated by literature focused on customer-facing initiatives, this book breaks new ground by addressing the challenges and opportunities of managing products designed not for external markets but for the people within your organization. Shifting the spotlight inward offers a fresh perspective on how internal tools can drive efficiency, foster innovation, and create value throughout the enterprise.

Managing internal products is a uniquely challenging and deeply rewarding facet of product management. While my focus has often been on external product management, I've had the privilege of working alongside colleagues deeply immersed in delivering internal products, witnessing firsthand their transformative power—and occasional pitfalls. This book is not just a guide; it's a thoughtful distillation of experiences, insights, and strategies that resonate deeply with the challenges many of us have faced.

As I read it, I was reminded of the years Ilana and I spent working together in a large financial institution's Enterprise Project Management Office. Those were intense learning years, where we found ourselves at the front lines of the battle to transform deeply ingrained command-and-control mindsets. Through every internal or customer-facing initiative, we championed adaptive ways of working, fostering strong product stewardship and an unwavering belief in employee agency. Our journey was marked by countless challenges and breakthroughs—moments that helped shape the principles and practices so effectively captured in this book.

1

Unlike external-facing initiatives, where metrics like market share and customer retention dominate, internal products require a keen understanding of the organization's pulse. They demand a balance between technical innovation and the pragmatic realities of budgets (sometimes very modest indeed), timelines, and the diverse needs of internal stakeholders. For Ilana and me, this often meant pushing boundaries while carefully nurturing trust and collaboration across teams—an art that this book so deftly explores.

While many of the insights draw deeply from Ilana's years of experience after our time with the same employer, some of the tales within these pages vividly rekindled memories of our adventures together. The stories of product managers navigating the labyrinth of internal tools echo the highs, lows, and lightbulb moments we experienced. Some are more whimsical, presumably protecting the innocent (or the guilty!), but all are relatable. Whether standing firm in the face of resistance or celebrating incremental wins that paved the way for more significant change, these moments taught us the power of persistence and empathy in driving transformation.

What makes this work particularly compelling is its grounding in reality. It doesn't shy away from the messy middle—the complexities of aligning stakeholder expectations, fostering a culture of collaboration, and balancing competing priorities. Instead, it offers actionable strategies, practical wisdom, and a dose of humour that feels like a trusted companion guiding you through the intricacies of internal product management.

If you, like Ilana and me, have spent sleepless nights wondering how to serve your teams better, bridge the gap between strategy and execution, or make sense of competing priorities, this book will feel like a conversation with a wise and experienced colleague. It's a resource I wish we'd had in those early days—a beacon for navigating the challenges and opportunities that define this unique field.

As you embark on or deepen your journey into internal product management, may this book inspire you to think differently, act decisively, and always keep your users—the people within your organization—at the heart of your efforts. Let's continue building not just better tools but better workplaces.

Daniel Gagnon
Organizational Adaptiveness Advisor
Creator of the Dynamic Value Curation™ approach

Preface

Inside the Box is designed for Product Managers who are accountable for internal products. You should already be familiar with the basics of product management before reading it. (If you aren't, see the references for some great books on the topic.)

This book focuses on software designed for internal use rather than for selling to external customers. While the core principles of traditional product management are preserved, the material is adapted to meet the unique challenges and requirements of managing products used within the organization. My goal is to provide practical, straightforward advice and strategies to develop effective, user-friendly internal software that aligns with organizational needs and goals. I hope you find it useful.

All stories contained within, while fanciful, are based on real-life experiences I have either seen first-hand or have had shared with me.

An Introduction to Internal
Product Management

Product management is the discipline of guiding a product through its lifecycle, from initial concept to delivery, ensuring it meets user needs and achieves business objectives. It involves a blend of strategic planning, user research, cross-functional collaboration, and iterative improvement. A Product Manager bridges the gap between stakeholders, development teams, and users, acting as the advocate for the product's vision and value.

When we talk about managing products internally, we're diving into a special area of product management that requires a special set of skills and know-how. Here, an internal Product Manager* is responsible for building, rolling out, and fine-tuning products meant for use within the organization. The aim is straightforward: to make operations smoother, boost productivity, and bring value to the business.

Internal products are the tools or services a company develops, mainly for its people or partners, not for the customers or the wider public. Think of things like internal software tools or intranet services—anything created to help with the company's internal workings.

So, what does a Product Manager for internal products do? The role is pivotal and primarily about understanding what the different teams and departments

---

*   Going forward from here, I will call the role Product Manager, but it is always in reference to one who is accountable for internally used software.

in the company need. Product Managers are the ones who spot places where a fantastic new tool or system could make things run smoothly and efficiently inside the company, making them an integral part of the company's operations.

It's very important to build a clear vision and strategy for the product. The Product Manager needs to ensure that what they're building fits with what the company wants to achieve. That means setting clear goals and figuring out the key results to aim for with the product.

Next up is planning out the product roadmap. This involves deciding which features to build and when, while always considering what will bring the most value and what's realistic to achieve. It's a bit of a juggling act, managing the various needs and wants of different people in the company.

Then there's working with the development teams. The Product Manager is the one who ensures everyone's on the same page about what needs to be built and that everything's up to scratch quality-wise. Their role is to keep things organized and clear up any uncertainties so the development can continue without a hitch, instilling confidence in the product's development.

Communication is key. The Product Manager needs to keep talking to people in the company, to get their feedback, and to keep them in the loop about updates and new releases. They also need to ensure everyone knows how to use the product and has the support they need.

Let's not forget about monitoring the product's performance. That means analyzing the data, observing how the product is being used, and determining where improvements can be made.

Success in this role often comes down to understanding the company and its people's needs, being a clear and effective communicator, and being decisive. A solid understanding of tech, how to build products, and what makes a good user experience is also necessary. And, of course, it's about keeping all the different plates spinning and managing priorities and resources effectively. You should see the similarities if you have a traditional product management background.

Ultimately, managing internal products is all about understanding the unique challenges within the company and finding smart solutions. The Product Manager is the go-to person to make sure internal products align with what the company needs and wants, helping to make everyone's life a bit easier and the company more efficient. By promoting a culture of collaboration and striving for excellence, Product Managers inspire and motivate others, helping drive innovation from the inside and paving the way for the company's ongoing success.

Differences between External and Internal Product Management

So, we've examined what it means to manage internal products, but you might wonder, "How is this different from managing products meant for customers?" Well, let's explore it.

	External Product Management	Internal Product Management
Adaptability	Adapt to market changes	Adapt to organizational changes
Resources	Higher budget and resources	Limited resources
Feedback	Various channels, mixed feedback	Direct from peers, real-time
Success Metrics	User acquisition, retention, revenue growth	User adoption, satisfaction
Goals	Increase market share, boost revenue, build brand	Efficiency and productivity
Focus	Market needs, customer feedback, competition	Team needs and workflows

Firstly, it's all about whom we are building for. External products are designed for our customers. We need them to love our products, so we're considering market needs, customer feedback, and competition. But for internal products, the game changes. We're building for our colleagues, focusing on the needs and workflow of our own teams. It's less about market trends and more about making our day-to-day tasks easier. This shift in focus presents unique challenges that we'll delve into.

The goals for external and internal products can be worlds apart. With external products, we often aim to increase market share, boost revenue, or build a brand reputation while satisfying our customers' needs. But when we're dealing with internal products, it's all about efficiency and productivity. We're creating tools that help our teams do their jobs better and faster, and that's a win in itself. (And don't forget, happy employees make happy customers.)

Success looks different, too. For external products, we're chasing metrics like user acquisition, retention, and revenue growth. We want to see those customer numbers going up. But for internal products, it's about user adoption and satisfaction within our teams. Are people actually using the tool? Is it making their work easier? That's what counts. Understanding these key metrics is crucial in managing internal products, ensuring you're informed and prepared for the challenges ahead.

Another area where things diverge is how we get feedback. When dealing with external products, customer feedback might come through various channels and can be a mix of praise and a laundry list of things to improve. However, with internal products, we're getting feedback directly from our peers, often in real time and sometimes over a coffee break. This means we can iterate and improve quickly, but it also means we must be ready for candid conversations.

Lastly, there's usually a difference in resources. External products often get the lion's share of the budget and team members because they bring in the revenue. Internal products, however, might need to make do with less. This means being resourceful and prioritizing like a pro to get the most out of what we have.

We often need to be more flexible and adaptive in managing internal products. User needs can change quickly as organizational needs evolve, and we must be ready to pivot. While external products also need to adapt to market changes, the changes in internal products can be more frequent and abrupt due to shifting internal priorities and immediate needs.

While there's some overlap, managing internal products is a different ball game. It's less about the market and more about our people. It's about understanding our colleagues' needs, solving internal challenges, and making the workplace more efficient and enjoyable. Whether dealing with different goals, measuring success differently, or navigating feedback from peers, Product Managers navigate a unique and rewarding path, helping to shape the environment in which we all work.

Importance of Internal Products in Today's Business Environment

We've talked about what internal product management is and how it differs from its external counterpart, but let's hit on why it's such a big deal in the business world today. Why should companies invest time, effort, and resources in building products that the outside world might never see? Here's the scoop:

Fueling Efficiency and Productivity

In today's fast-paced business world, every minute counts. Internal products are the unsung heroes that keep things running smoothly behind the scenes. They help automate mundane tasks, reduce errors, and save time, allowing everyone to focus on what they do best. When teams spend less time on the extraneous and more on their core work, it's a win-win for productivity and job satisfaction (Colotla et al., 2024).

Driving Innovation from Within

Internal products are a hotbed for innovation. They encourage teams to think outside the box and develop new solutions to internal challenges. This culture of innovation doesn't just stay within; it spills over, fostering a mindset of continuous improvement and creative problem-solving that benefits every part of the business (Koch et al., 2013).

Enhancing Decision-Making

Data is king, and internal products are the royal carriers. By providing accurate and timely data, internal tools empower teams to make informed decisions fast. This means less guessing and more data-driven choices—crucial in staying ahead in the competitive business landscape.

Boosting Employee Morale and Retention

Let's be honest—working with outdated, clunky tools can be a drag. When companies invest in sleek, user-friendly internal products, it shows they care about their employees' experiences. This not only makes the daily grind more enjoyable but also plays a significant role in keeping great talent around (Stein, 2021).

Adapting to Change

The business world is always changing, and companies need to keep up. Internal products allow for quick adaptation to new industry trends, market shifts, or changes in company strategy. Whether it's a sudden shift to remote work or a new market opportunity, having the right tools in place makes rolling with the punches much easier.

Reducing Costs in the Long Run

It might seem like a big upfront investment, but well-designed internal products can save companies a lot of money in the long run. By streamlining processes and reducing the need for manual work, internal products help cut operational costs and free up resources for other important initiatives.

Ultimately, internal products might not get the spotlight, but they're crucial in building a successful, modern business. They're the silent engines driving efficiency, innovation, and smart decision-making, helping companies navigate the complexities of the business world. Whether it's about keeping employees happy or staying agile in a sea of changes, investing in internal products is not just smart—it's essential for survival in today's cutthroat business environment.

Tales of the Product Manager

Once upon a time, in the land of Corporate Conglomerates, there was a company named Speedy Solutions. Speedy Solutions was known for its sleek, sophisticated external products. But internally? Well, that was a different story. The internal tools were like a pair of old, worn-out shoes—functional but not the most comfortable or stylish.

Here's where our hero, Pat, the Product Manager, steps in. Pat was assigned to revamp the internal tool that everyone used, and everyone loathed. It was called "Slo-Mo," given its ability to make simple tasks last an eternity.

Pat rolled up their sleeves and dived in. They gathered feedback from every corner of the company, and the consensus was clear—everyone wanted Slo-Mo to be more like "Go-Go." Pat worked tirelessly with the development team, transforming Slo-Mo from a sluggish snail into a sprightly cheetah. The transformation was anything but smooth, with lots of coffee, heated discussions, and a few "lightbulb" moments.

When the new and improved Slo-Mo was finally rolled out, it was met with a standing ovation (and a few tears of joy) from the employees. Gone were the days of twiddling thumbs, waiting for pages to load, and juggling between ten tabs to perform one simple task.

But here's the funny part: the overhaul was so successful that the rumour mill started churning out stories about the magical powers of the revamped Slo-Mo. Some swore it could predict the weather, while others believed it could brew coffee. Soon, employees from other companies were knocking on Speedy Solutions' door, wanting a piece of the magical Slo-Mo.

Despite Slo-Mo's newfound fame and rumoured magical abilities, Pat had to politely explain that it was just an internal tool designed to make life at

Speedy Solutions a bit more . . . speedy. Pat's mission was accomplished, and they had not only upgraded an internal tool but also unknowingly created a corporate legend in the process.

Effective internal product management plays a pivotal role and can have a tremendous impact. It's not just about creating a functional tool; it's about improving the work life of every employee in the company and, sometimes, creating a bit of magic along the way.

Points to Ponder

 How does your approach to internal product management reflect the unique needs of your organization? Reflect on how well your strategies align with your company's goals and culture.

 What are the most significant challenges you face in managing internal products? Consider how these challenges differ from those in external product management.

 In what ways do you measure the success of your internal products? Think about the metrics and feedback mechanisms you currently use and how they might be improved.

Understanding Your
Internal Customers

Understanding your internal users is crucial because it's a roadmap to creating successful products. If you don't know who you're building for and what they need, you're essentially navigating blind.

When you take the time to profile your internal stakeholders and users, you are putting yourself in their shoes and seeing the world from their perspective. It's about acknowledging that every department, team, and individual has unique needs and challenges. Understanding these unique needs helps tailor the product to suit them best, ensuring better adoption and smoother implementation.

If Product Managers ignore this step, they risk creating products that may look good on paper but are of no real use to those needing them. They also risk wasting valuable resources. It's like cooking a meal without knowing your guests' dietary restrictions and preferences. You might end up with a great-looking dish, but no one's going to eat it.

By profiling internal stakeholders and users, Product Managers are not just building a bridge between what's needed and what's created, they are the architects of this bridge. They ensure that the products developed are not just relevant but are also valuable, user-friendly, and effective in solving the day-to-day challenges faced by the users within the organization. In simple terms, it's about making sure that what you build actually makes a difference to the people using it.

To enhance our understanding of internal customers, building detailed personas is an essential step. Personas are semi-fictional characters based on your real users that help product teams understand user needs, experiences, behaviours, and goals. By crafting these personas, teams can visualize and empathize with the users they are creating products for, leading to more targeted and effective solutions. To create a persona, you must:

1. Gather quantitative and qualitative data from user interactions, feedback, surveys, and interviews.

2. Identify common attributes among users, such as roles, goals, challenges, and behaviours, to group similar users together.

3. Develop detailed personas that include demographic information, job roles, needs, pain points, preferences, and typical-day scenarios.

4. Use these personas during ideation sessions to guide feature development and ensure alignment with real user needs.

Imagine a persona named "Chris," a mid-level manager who regularly uses the internal project management tool. Chris struggles with efficiently allocating resources across projects due to the tool's cumbersome interface. Understanding Chris's daily challenges and needs can guide the development team to prioritize enhancements in the tool's resource allocation features.

Using personas helps ensure that the products developed are not only technically sound but that they also deeply resonate with users and are useful to them. It prevents the common disconnect that occurs when developers are isolated from the actual users of their products.

Collecting Internal Feedback

Knowing your internal users is a game-changer, and collecting their feedback is like getting the secret-sauce recipe for your product. One tried-and-true method is good, old-fashioned conversation. Grab a coffee, sit down with your users, and chat. It's relaxed, it's informal, and you'd be surprised how much you can learn when people are at ease and speak freely.

Now, for a chuckle, consider the tale of a Product Manager—let's call him Joe—who wanted to gather feedback on a new tool his team was developing. Instead of setting up formal meetings, Joe posted an invitation for a "Mystery Lunch"—a free meal with an unknown agenda. The curiosity was too much for the team, and people from different departments showed up, eager for a free bite and a bit of intrigue.

Once the group was settled with sandwiches and salads, Joe unveiled his true motive: a sneak peek at the new tool. The room was filled with a mix of amusement and playful groans. After the initial surprise, the atmosphere buzzed with lively discussions and constructive feedback. Joe not only collected diverse insights but also turned a routine feedback session into a memorable experience, reinforcing the idea that collecting feedback can be engaging and fun.

Beyond the creative and the casual, don't underestimate the power of structured approaches like surveys and questionnaires. Clear, concise, and to the point, they allow users to provide their thoughts and insights in their own time, making them convenient and user-friendly. It's like having a suggestion box—some of the ideas might be off the wall, but hidden among them could be the gem that takes your product to the next level.

Remember, collecting internal feedback isn't a chore—it's an adventure, filled with discoveries, laughs, and the occasional curveball. It's about getting to the heart of what your users need and want, allowing you to tailor your product in a way that makes a difference. Whether through a casual chat over coffee, a surprise lunch, or a well-crafted survey, every piece of feedback is a step toward creating a product that truly meets the needs of your internal stakeholders. Keep it light, keep it engaging, and watch the insights roll in.

Conversational Feedback

Starting with a casual conversation can be like striking gold for insights. It's perfect when you're fleshing out new ideas and want those raw, unfiltered thoughts. But beware, people might not spill all the beans if they have negative things to share, and if you don't steer the conversation right, you might end up with a lot of unclear or broad feedback.

Example:

Alex, a Product Manager, joins departmental meetings to discuss enhancements for a project tracking tool. Through these discussions, Alex discovers a need for a mobile app to allow quick status updates, leading to its development and increased user adoption.

Surveys and Questionnaires

Sending out surveys is like casting a wide net; it's your go-to when you need to hear from a bigger, diverse group, and when you crave those structured, quantifiable insights to guide your decision-making. But be cautious; a poorly framed survey is a recipe for disaster and can lead to misleading or useless data. Not only that, getting people to take a survey can be a struggle.

Example:

 At SpeedyTech, surveys about the internal communication platform highlighted a high demand for integrating instant-messaging and video-conferencing features. This feedback adjusted the product roadmap to prioritize these features, aligning development with user needs.

Feedback Boxes or Suggestion Boxes

Having a feedback box can be a mixed bag: some feedback might be a puzzle without enough context, and some might just be not helpful at all. But a feedback box is like having a secret window into the minds of your users, where they can drop their thoughts anonymously and continuously.

Example:

 A multinational introduces a digital suggestion box, uncovering not only small issues but also a significant gap in the internal reporting tools. This leads to a redesign that better aligns the tools with actual workflows, increasing efficiency.

Focus Groups

Conducting focus groups is akin to assembling a mini-orchestra of diverse voices, each contributing to the symphony of insights on specific topics. Do be aware, though, that conducting focus groups requires a knack for balance; a dominant voice can overshadow the others, and aligning everyone's schedules can be quite the juggling act.

Example:

 A focus group at an e-commerce company reveals that while their new inventory management system is functional for most departments, logistics struggles with its interface. This feedback prompts the creation of a tailored interface for logistics, significantly enhancing usability.

Usability Tests

Watching users interact with your product through usability tests can unveil hidden challenges in the user experience. It's critical when you want to identify friction points in user interactions with your product. But remember, being watched can make people act differently, and their actions under observation might not truly reflect their natural interactions with the product.

Example:

At a small software company, the product team conducted usability tests on their new task management tool. Observing team members using the tool, they discovered that the process of assigning tasks was overly complicated, leading to confusion and errors. Based on this insight, they simplified the interface, significantly improving the tool's usability and user satisfaction.

Mixing and matching these methods often yields the most rounded, insightful results, allowing you to tailor your product to your users' needs and wishes. The following table summarizes your options, as well as both pros and cons. Keep your approach simple and direct, and let the insights flow.

Method	Description	Advantages	Disadvantages
Conversational Feedback	Casual, relaxed, good for new ideas but might lack depth in negative feedback.	Strikes gold for insights; perfect for fleshing out new ideas.	Might get unclear or broad feedback and might not get deep negative feedback.
Surveys and Questionnaires	Broad reach, structured insights.	Wide net, structured insights; guides decision-making.	Poorly framed = disaster; might struggle to get participation; risk of poor data if not well designed.
Feedback Boxes	Anonymous, continuous input.	Secret window into user minds; continuous feedback.	Mixed bag; some feedback not helpful or puzzling; may lack context.
Focus Groups	Diverse insights on specific topics.	Mini-orchestra of diverse voices; specific topic insights.	Dominant voice can overshadow; scheduling issues.
Usability Tests	Identifies user interaction friction.	Unveils hidden challenges; critical for identifying friction points.	Watched behaviour might not reflect true interactions.

Want more?

If you've already tried a combination of the above techniques but are still left wondering what else you could have done, you might want to tap into the "wisdom of crowds" using Liberating Structures. There are over 35 tried-and-true techniques documented here:

https://www.liberatingstructures.com/

Some of the better-known (and most effective) Liberating Structures include 1-2-4 All, What I need From You, and Open Space.

Addressing Diverse Needs Within Your Organization

Addressing diverse needs while supporting internal software demands a balanced and empathetic approach. Start by acknowledging the variety of needs, preferences, and expectations within the organization. This recognition makes every department, every team, and every individual feel recognized and understood, as their interactions with the software will reflect this diversity. It's crucial to cultivate an environment of open communication where users feel heard and understood and believe that their feedback is valued and acted upon.

Prioritize active listening and seek to understand different stakeholders' underlying needs and concerns. It's not about finding a one-size-fits-all solution but about identifying common ground and building flexible, adaptable solutions catering to a spectrum of needs and preferences. A helpful approach is to establish clear channels for feedback and maintain transparency about the development process and any constraints, so stakeholders have realistic expectations and understand the rationale behind product decisions.

Consider this situation:

Alex, a Product Manager, introduces a new feature in the company's financial reporting software. The accounting team warmly welcomes the feature, which makes their financial tracking and reporting tasks much smoother. However, the marketing team finds the feature cumbersome, complicating their expense reporting.

To navigate this, Alex sets up a meeting with members from both teams to better understand their needs and apprehensions. The marketing team voices their concerns about the feature making their interface cluttered and complicated, whereas the accounting team explains how it optimizes their workflow by reducing manual work.

Alex recognizes the diverse needs and suggests a solution allowing individual users to turn the feature on or off according to their preferences. This ensures the accounting team can use the feature to its fullest, enhancing their productivity, while at the same time, the marketing team can keep their interface clean and focused, avoiding any perceived additional complexity.

Recognizing, respecting, and accommodating the distinct needs and preferences of different teams builds a harmonious organizational atmosphere where each voice is heard and cultivates a more inclusive environment in which each concern is addressed.

Points to Ponder

 How well do you know the pain points of your internal customers? Consider the steps you can take to deepen your understanding of their daily challenges.

 Are you actively engaging with your internal stakeholders? Reflect on the methods you use to gather their input. Could there be more effective ways to involve them in the product development process?

 How do you ensure that the products you develop are aligned with the actual needs of internal users? What checks and balances are in place to validate these needs?

Establishing Clear Objectives

I n product management, clear objectives are akin to steering a ship with a known destination. Objectives are the compass that ensures you don't get lost at sea. Objectives illuminate the path, creating a shared sense of purpose and setting a standard to gauge progress and success. They're crucial because they provide a coherent direction, aligning every task and every effort with a common goal and creating a roadmap to the desired outcome. It's about setting not just any goals but the right ones that align with the overall vision of your organization.

Without clear objectives, teams can easily drift off course, efforts become disjointed, and resources may be squandered in the wrong places. Whether short-term or long-term, well-defined objectives guarantee every endeavour is a step toward meaningful accomplishments. They prevent the dispersion of focus and resources, ensuring each task performed is a brick in building the organization's success.

Moreover, objectives should not stand isolated; they should connect and contribute to the organization's broader goals. If there's a misalignment, it's like rowing a boat against the current; a lot of energy is expended, but progress is minimal. Proper alignment with organizational goals ensures that every product strategy and every effort is harmoniously intertwined with the bigger organizational picture, pulling the entire entity in the intended direction.

This alignment also brings coherence within teams. It's the glue that binds every team member, creating a synergy where everyone is moving in unison toward common objectives. Understanding the "why" behind each task enriches motivation, fosters collaboration, and bolsters morale, making the journey as rewarding as the destination.

Well-defined and aligned objectives act as a lighthouse in the often-foggy product development journey. It's not merely about charting the path but ensuring that every step taken is constructing the organization's envisioned future. It's this alignment that makes every project, effort, and resource expended a meaningful contribution to the organization's success story. With a clear destination and a coherent roadmap, teams can sail the turbulent waters of product management with a renewed sense of purpose and confidence, translating visions into tangible achievements.

Tales of the Product Manager

Once upon a time, in the bustling realm of CorpWorld, a team of gallant Developers, Designers, and Product Managers known as the Code Knights embarked on a mission to create a marvellous piece of procurement software. The software was to simplify the lives of their fellow CorpWorld inhabitants and be the key to the harmonious coexistence of spreadsheets, purchase orders, and supplier negotiations.

However, the Code Knights were a bit too engrossed in their individual quests, each battling their own dragons and chasing their own grails, neglecting the ancient scroll of "Alignment and Clear Objectives." The result? A piece of software that was more of a labyrinth than a solution, where users would wander aimlessly, grappling with the Minotaur of confusing features and the Sirens of unnecessary buttons.

The inhabitants of CorpWorld were in despair. The Finance Wizards couldn't make sense of the cumbersome invoice features, the Supply Chain Sorcerers were lost in the maze of supplier data, and the Procurement Elves were tangled in the vines of complex order forms.

Realizing that chaos had ensued, the Code Knights gathered around the Round Table, laying down their arms and shields to mend the fractured alignment and reinstate harmony. They embarked on a noble quest of listening, understanding, and reflecting, ensuring every voice was heard and every concern was addressed.

With their newfound wisdom, the Code Knights reforged the procurement software, each stroke of the keyboard and click of the mouse echoing CorpWorld's unified heartbeat. They intertwined the needs of Finance Wizards with the desires of Supply Chain Sorcerers and the preferences of Procurement Elves, creating a seamless orchestration of features and functionalities that harmonized with the symphony of user satisfaction.

The reforged software became the beacon of hope and efficiency in CorpWorld, a testament to the magic of alignment and the power of collaboration. The inhabitants could now navigate the procurement paths with ease and joy, with the once-cumbersome processes transformed into a dance of clicks and scrolls.

And the Code Knights, with their armour shining brighter and their bonds stronger, rode into the sunset, leaving behind the legacy of aligned objectives and harmonious solutions, whispering in the winds the tales of unity, understanding, and the pursuit of user happiness.

Thus, the CorpWorld inhabitants lived happily ever after, with procurement woes a mere shadow of the past, all thanks to the united spirits of the Code Knights and the enchanted software that brought prosperity and peace to the land of CorpWorld.

Short-Term and Long-Term Objectives

When crafting software, think of objectives as the stepping stones that lead us to our ultimate destination. It's essential to lay down both short-term and long-term stones to form a complete path to success. Short-term objectives are like the sparks that ignite immediate action and fuel the momentum. They energize and focus the team, allowing us to make consistent progress. Long-term objectives, however, are the north stars guiding us through our journey, ensuring that every step we take is in the right direction toward our grand vision.

There's a time and place for each objective. Short-term objectives are great when we need to solve immediate challenges or start a new project. They help in breaking down a monumental task into manageable chunks, making the journey seem less overwhelming. Long-term objectives are the companions for the long haul, necessary when we're aiming for substantial, transformative changes or creating something revolutionary.

When we set these objectives, it's not about just putting them out there and hoping for the best. It's about creating actionable, attainable goals and developing a clear strategy to achieve them. We need to break down our objectives into smaller tasks, allocate adequate resources, and establish realistic timelines.

Measuring our progress is like checking the compass regularly to ensure we're on the right path. We can use both qualitative and quantitative objectives for this. Quantitative objectives are the numbers and stats that give us clear, tangible targets and help us measure our progress accurately. They're like the mile markers telling us exactly how far we've come and how far we need to go.

On the other hand, qualitative objectives are the less tangible, more experiential goals. They're about the quality of the journey, the learnings we acquire, and the relationships we build along the way. They help us understand the impact of our work on the users, the experiences we're creating, and the value we're adding.

For instance, if we're developing a feature to enhance user satisfaction, a quantitative objective could be reducing the number of support tickets by 30% within two months. A qualitative objective could be receiving positive feedback and improved user testimonials regarding the enhanced user experience.

In essence, having both short- and long-term objectives, measuring them appropriately, and understanding the nuances of qualitative and quantitative objectives help create a balanced approach, ensuring not just the achievement of goals but also the enrichment of the journey. By juggling these different facets adeptly, we can navigate our ship smoothly, making the journey as rewarding as reaching the destination.

By combining clear goals with the right way to check our progress, we ensure we're on the right path and use our time and energy where it matters most.

Measures are the compass needles that help us stay true to our course, and they're vital because they enable us to prioritize our work effectively. When we know exactly where we stand and where we need to go, it becomes easier to allocate our time, energy, and resources to the truly essential tasks that drive us forward the most efficiently.

However, it's critical to choose the right measures. It's tempting to focus on shiny "vanity measures" that look impressive on paper but don't really contribute to our true north. Vanity measures are like mirages. They may look appealing, but they don't offer real value. They might give us a temporary sense of achievement but can lead us astray from our true objectives.

Choosing the right measures is about focusing on what truly matters, what truly drives us toward our goals. It's about aligning our measures with our fundamental, meaningful objectives and avoiding the allure of superficial success. Concentrating on significant, impactful measures ensures that every step we take is a step in the right direction, bringing us closer to our true destination.

Points to Ponder

 Are your product objectives clearly defined and communicated to all stakeholders? Reflect on how well these objectives align with your organization's overall goals.

 How do you balance short-term and long-term objectives in your product strategy? Consider the impact of this balance on your product's development and success.

 What processes are in place to measure progress toward your objectives? Think about whether these processes are sufficient and how they could be enhanced.

The Product
Management Lifecycle

T
he Product Management Lifecycle is a comprehensive frame-work that guides a product's successful creation, launch, and evolution, ensuring it aligns with business goals and meets customer needs. Its purpose is to provide a structured approach to product development, enabling organizations to strategically plan, prioritize, and execute product initiatives. The Product Management Lifecycle ultimately supports informed decision-making, efficient resource allocation, and a customer-centric approach to product development.

Ideation/Iteration

Brainstorming new product ideas and identifying improvement opportunities.

Continuous ideation and iteration serve as the cornerstones for product evolution, especially for products intended for internal use. This emphasis is crucial because internal products must adapt quickly to an organization's ever-changing needs and processes. Unlike products designed for external markets, which may prioritize broad market trends and customer acquisition, internal products must align closely with the specific operational efficiencies and employee workflows. As such, continuously revising these products based on real-time feedback and internal user insights ensures they remain functional, relevant, and beneficial over time.

Strategic Ideation Techniques

To foster a culture of continuous improvement, it is essential to employ structured ideation techniques. One effective method is conducting cross-functional ideation workshops that bring together diverse teams from across the organization. These workshops should utilize creative problem-solving frameworks like Design Thinking, which encourages empathy with end-users and open-ended problem exploration. For example, using persona-based scenarios during these workshops can help teams step into the shoes of various internal users, leading to insights that drive more targeted and effective iterations.

Leveraging Technology for Iterative Feedback

Incorporating technology like rapid prototyping tools allows teams to quickly iterate on ideas and receive immediate feedback. Tools such as digital whiteboards or software that simulate user interactions can be used to create prototypes that get tested and tweaked in real time. This approach speeds up the iteration cycle and helps visualize solutions and refine them based on direct stakeholder input.

Comparative Analysis for Continuous Improvement

Additionally, incorporating a comparative analysis of past iterations can provide valuable insights. Regularly reviewing and comparing the outcomes of previous iterations helps identify patterns and trends that indicate success or highlight recurring challenges. For instance, tracking each iteration's adoption rate and user-satisfaction metrics can shed light on which changes had the most positive impact and which areas still need improvement.

By perpetually refining the product based on dynamic needs and insights acquired from internal users, we ensure the sustained relevance and value of the product within the organizational context. This process begins with organizing structured ideation workshops that bring together cross-functional teams to break down silos and stimulate creativity through diverse insights.

For example, if a team is developing an internal communication tool, continuous brainstorming sessions might lead to the realization that users require more seamless integration with other internal tools or may desire additional features such as document sharing or integrated scheduling. Recognizing and responding to such insights would allow the product to evolve in alignment with user needs, maintaining its intrinsic value to the organization. This iterative approach is more than a methodology; it is a culture of relentless enhancement and innovation. It embeds a mindset of perpetual improvement within the team, pushing the boundaries of what the product can achieve and driving it to new heights of efficiency and utility.

By embracing this culture, we not only improve the product but also enrich the work environment, fostering a proactive and innovative approach to problem-solving. Frequent and direct interaction with internal users is crucial in this process. Regular feedback sessions, surveys, or even informal conversations can reveal pain points, unmet needs, and opportunities for improvement that may not be evident otherwise. For instance, while the original specifications of a financial reporting tool may have met the initial needs of the finance department, regular interactions may reveal the necessity for more advanced data analysis capabilities or customization options to accommodate varying reporting needs across different teams.

By incorporating feedback, we not only fine-tune the existing features but also uncover avenues for innovation, identifying areas that warrant attention in subsequent development cycles. This could involve enhancing the existing functionalities, adding new features, or even reimagining certain aspects of the product to better align with the evolving user needs.

Integration of Agile Methodologies

To further enhance our ideation and iteration efforts, integrating agile methodologies can significantly increase the responsiveness and adaptability of our processes. By organizing ideation into structured time blocks, using Kanban boards for visual management of ideas, and holding regular meetings to assess progress, we can maintain a rhythmic flow of innovation. These agile practices help in quickly identifying what works and what doesn't, allowing teams to pivot as needed and keep the innovation pipeline fresh and relevant. This structured yet flexible approach ensures that every idea is given due consideration and that the most promising ones are developed rapidly in response to user feedback and evolving market needs.

Through the fusion of consistent ideation and iterative refinement, steered by direct user insights, we can cultivate a product that aligns with the current organizational landscape and is poised to adapt and thrive in the face of future evolutions. By embracing this approach, we lay the foundation for a product that is resilient, relevant, and perpetually attuned to the pulse of the organization's needs.

However, as with any method or approach, there are problems to look out for. The following table highlights the more common issues.

Problem	Description	Signs	Solution
Over-iteration	Iterating excessively without significant enhancements or progress.	Product cycles extend without clear improvements; minor tweaks do not significantly enhance product value.	Set specific objectives for each iteration cycle. Use decision-making frameworks to ensure timely progress and avoid continuous minor adjustments.
Under-iteration	Insufficient iteration leading to unresolved use issues or use defects.	Consistent use feedback on the same issues; new features released with defects.	Implement robust feedback loops. Include user testing and real-time usage data to inform and validate each iteration.
Unfeasible Ideation	Ideation sessions consistently produce impractical or overly ambitious ideas.	Ideas regularly exceed technical capabilities or budget; lack of practical grounding.	Define technical, budgetary, and time constraints before ideation. Use feasibility studies and involve cross-functional teams early in the process.
Novelty Trap	Focusing on innovation for its own sake without adding real user or business value.	Ideas are innovative but do not align with user needs or business objectives.	Use tools like a value proposition canvas to ensure ideas address real user pain points or business needs. Revisit user personas and journey maps regularly.
Lack of Diverse Perspectives	Ideation lacks varied inputs, leading to repetitive or uninspired ideas.	Ideas lack variety or innovation: feedback from the same group dynamics.	Involve diverse stakeholders in ideation sessions, including different departments' user groups and external experts, to ensure a range of perspectives.

Market Research

Understanding the needs and wants of your target audience

Creating a product for internal users does have the advantage of a shared understanding of users and business goals since we know who the users are and what the business intends to achieve. However, it's imperative to recognize that the absence of traditional competitors does not negate the need for meticulous market research and competitive analysis.

While external market research often focuses on understanding customer needs and competitor offerings, internal product market research faces its own set of challenges. One of the key challenges is the lack of external benchmarks. Unlike external products, internal products do not typically have direct competitors, making it harder to gauge how well your solution meets user needs compared to other options.

Another challenge is the potential for bias in feedback. Since internal users are part of the same organization, they may be more reluctant to criticize a product or may express needs based on familiarity with current processes rather than on optimal solutions. This can lead to under-reporting of issues or over-optimism about the current system's effectiveness.

Additionally, internal products often have to balance the needs of multiple departments or user groups, each with different priorities. This can complicate the research process, as it requires gathering and analyzing data from a diverse range of stakeholders with varying expectations and workflows.

Compare the features of your internal product with those of commercially available tools, even if the latter are external products. This can highlight potential areas for improvement or spur innovation in your internal product. There are several different approaches to a Feature Gap Analysis, from a simple checklist to a SWOT Analysis, Journey Mapping, Feature Mapping, or Benchmarking.

Studying the tools and systems employed by organizations of a similar nature can be enlightening. Analyzing commercially available tools used by peer organizations for comparable functions can also offer insights into beneficial features, optimal usability, and efficient workflows, which could be incorporated to enhance the efficacy of the internal product.

Moreover, evaluating alternative solutions currently in use within the organization is necessary. For example, understanding the reliance on spreadsheets, manual processes, or third-party software to address similar needs can guide the development of a product that offers superior value and efficiency.

Staying abreast of technological advancements is also vital. This could involve exploring new software frameworks, automation tools, or data-analysis methods that could significantly improve the functionality and user experience of the internal product.

Reviewing past solutions and assessing their successes and shortcomings can provide valuable lessons. For example, a retrospective analysis of a previously used project-management tool can reveal underutilized features or design aspects that users found cumbersome, thereby making the new design more user-friendly and functional.

Lastly, conducting a thorough cost-benefit analysis is indispensable. Comparing the economic and operational aspects of developing an internal product versus adopting a commercial one ensures the chosen solution is viable and offers the organization's best value proposition. For example, the choice between developing a custom financial reporting tool and adopting a SaaS solution would hinge on an in-depth evaluation of the long-term value each brings to the organization.

Method	Description	When to Use	Outcome
Checklist Comparison	A simple, side-by-side comparison of features from both software products.	Use when you need a straightforward comparison of feature sets.	A clear visual representation of feature presence or absence.
SWOT Analysis	Analyzes strengths, weaknesses, opportunities, and threats for each software.	Use when you need a strategic overview of software capabilities.	A structured understanding of strengths, weaknesses, and gaps.
User Journey Mapping	Maps out the user experience across different stages of interaction with the software.	Use when understanding the user experience is critical.	A detailed view of how each software supports the user journey.
Feature Mapping	Visual representation of features, categorized and connected to show relationships and gaps.	Use when you need a visual tool to compare feature sets.	A visual map highlighting missing functionalities and overlaps.
Benchmarking	Compares software features against industry standards or leading competitors.	Use when comparing software against industry norms or competitors.	A comparison of software against benchmarks, identifying gaps.

Product Strategy and Roadmap

Defining the vision and strategic direction of the product.

Having a clear and well-articulated vision, coupled with a strategic direction, is pivotal, especially in the context of internal software development. It serves as the guiding light, ensuring every development step is in harmony with the overarching business goals, and consistently adds value to internal stakeholders. For example, if an organization is crafting a proprietary data-management tool, the vision and strategic direction should resonate with the enterprise's objectives of data optimization and streamlined access for various internal units.

A well-defined roadmap is the manifestation of this vision and strategic direction. It meticulously outlines the trajectory of the product, detailing the planned features and enhancements. This isn't just a timeline of development milestones; it's a communication tool that provides clarity and transparency to all relevant parties. For instance, elucidating the release of new features in an internal CRM system allows various departments to prepare and adapt their workflows accordingly, thereby reducing friction during implementation.

In internal software development, setting expectations through a clear roadmap is vital. It mitigates ambiguity and fosters an environment of trust and collaboration between the development team and the end-users. When stakeholders can visually comprehend the planned evolution of the product, it nurtures a sense of involvement and shared ownership, bridging the gap between development and usage.

Much of the market research completed in the previous stage of the product lifecycle is leveraged here, as you use the data gathered to prioritize features based on user needs, potential impact, and ease of implementation. For example, if a common pain point across departments is the difficulty of data entry in the current system, improving this feature should be a top priority.

Budgeting and resource allocation are integral components of this phase. The strategic vision must be anchored in reality, ensuring that the aspirations for the product are achievable within the constraints of available resources. Whether it's allocating developer hours or managing financial investments for the software, meticulous assessment and allocation of resources are indispensable to avoid overcommitments and ensure the smooth progression of the product through its lifecycle stages.

Change management becomes crucial from this phase because every new feature or enhancement could necessitate alterations in workflows and processes. Anticipating the organizational shifts induced by the product and strategizing for smooth integration is critical. For instance, introducing a new automation feature in an internal project management tool might necessitate training sessions for the staff and adjustments in how project timelines are managed, ensuring that the transition is smooth and the organization can reap the benefits of the new feature swiftly.

In essence, the strategy and roadmap phase is not just about plotting the course but about foreseeing the intricacies of the journey. It's about constructing a coherent narrative around the product's evolution, ensuring alignment with business objectives, managing resources efficiently, and paving the way for seamless integration of the product enhancements, thereby consolidating the foundation for a product that is poised to fulfill the dynamic needs of the internal stakeholders efficiently and effectively.

Alignment with Enterprise Architecture

Before delving into product definition and design, it's necessary to ensure that the product strategy is fully aligned with the organization's enterprise architecture. This alignment helps to clarify what technological and data resources are available and how they can be used within the new product. It also ensures that the product will fit seamlessly within the broader IT infrastructure, adhering to established standards and practices.

It may seem like an extra step or "too much governance," but before designing you need to:

- Align with Enterprise Frameworks: Before defining any product features or design elements, consult the enterprise architecture documentation and the team responsible for its maintenance. Understand the existing IT landscape, including hardware, software, network infrastructure, and data protocols.

- Comply with Data Requirements: Determine how the product will access and use data within the organization's framework. Ensure that the product adheres to data governance standards and compliance requirements, often part of the enterprise architecture.

- Synchronize Technology: Align the product's technological stack and deployment strategies with the existing setups. This involves selecting programming languages, development platforms, and deployment environments that are supported and scalable within the existing IT architecture.

At this point, you may be wondering why you need to do all that—it is an internal product, and the team just wants something to use. But there are several reasons:

- Efficiency in Development: By aligning the product strategy with the enterprise architecture at the outset, the development process becomes more streamlined, avoiding rework and ensuring faster delivery.

- Enhanced Security and Compliance: Early integration helps identify and incorporate necessary security features and compliance measures, reducing potential risks and vulnerabilities.

- Optimized Resource Utilization: Understanding the existing enterprise architecture allows for better utilization of current IT assets and infrastructure, potentially lowering development costs and improving ROI.

With a clear understanding of the enterprise architecture's impact on the product strategy, you can now define and design the product with confidence that it will integrate well into the organizational ecosystem.

Product Definition and Design

Specifying what the product will look like, its features, and how it will function.

Crafting a clear product definition and deliberate design is akin to laying the architectural plans for a building. Just as an architect wouldn't dream of constructing without detailed blueprints, Product Managers and developers shouldn't commence without a solid, well-outlined product specification. Think of enterprise resource planning (ERP) software: if the design doesn't categorically specify how each module interacts or fails to detail the user interface, the resulting software could be a labyrinth, difficult for employees to navigate and integrate into their daily operations.

By clearly defining what the product will look like, its salient features, and its functionality, the team is setting a precise course. This doesn't just give developers a clear picture of the end goal; it also significantly reduces the possibility of detours and missteps. A tangible benefit is the notable reduction in ambiguity. When developers know the exact shades of blue they should paint with, there's less room for error and fewer occasions where they might need to go back and repaint sections, metaphorically speaking. This foresight can lead to substantial savings, both in time and costs.

Continuing with our analogy of a building, people need to know how to move within it, where each section is, and how to use the facilities once it's constructed. Similarly, for a product, especially an internal software tool, user training and onboarding become pivotal. It's not just about building the software; it's about ensuring that each organization member can leverage its capabilities to the fullest. Imagine introducing a new inventory-management feature in an ERP system. Without proper training modules or onboarding processes, users might underutilize the tool or, worse, make errors that could lead to inventory discrepancies.

Additionally, the spectre of security threats looms large in today's increasingly digital landscape. This concern is amplified for internal tools, which often deal with sensitive, proprietary data. Consequently, as part of the design and definition phase, it is imperative to incorporate robust security measures. And it's not just about warding off external threats. Ensuring that there are levels of access where only authorized individuals can access certain data segments is crucial. Coupled with security is the aspect of compliance. Especially in sectors like finance or health care, meeting organizational and legal standards isn't optional; it's mandatory. Designing with these considerations in mind ensures the product serves its functional purpose, stands up to scrutiny, and safeguards the organization's integrity.

Product definition and design isn't just a preparatory phase. It's the compass and the map, ensuring that the journey is not just embarked upon with clarity but that it progresses efficiently, culminating in a product that aligns with organizational goals, user expectations, and broader compliance and security standards.

Launch

Planning the product launch and crafting adoption strategies.

When launching a new product, especially one designed to be used internally, think of it as introducing a new species into an ecosystem. It must adapt, coexist, and eventually flourish in its new environment. The ecosystem here is the organization, and all the existing processes, workflows, and tools are the inhabitants with which the new product must synergize. For instance, introducing a new data analytics tool involves not only the seamless integration of the tool itself but also the adaptation of employees to the new workflows it brings.

A meticulous launch plan is akin to preparing the ground. It's about ensuring that the introduction of this new entity is harmonious, causing minimal disruptions while maximizing synergies. Crafting astute adoption strategies is equivalent to ensuring that this new species can thrive and contribute to the ecosystem's overall health and productivity. For example, if a company is launching a new internal communication tool, careful planning around its rollout, coupled with strategies to encourage its use, such as tutorials or incentive programs, can ensure higher adoption rates and smoother integration into daily workflows.

A vital part of the launch phase is also anticipating and preparing for the post-launch scenario. The transition of a product into its live environment is rarely without its hiccups. Immediate post-launch support and maintenance are crucial in addressing emergent concerns or issues, ensuring users' continued satisfaction and confidence in the product. Suppose a newly launched HR software has a minor glitch in the leave application feature. Quick, effective support can address user concerns, fix the issue, and maintain user trust in the product.

Even as the product is launched and starts its journey in the organizational ecosystem, the foresight into its eventual retirement or transition is integral. It's about understanding that every product has a lifecycle, and being prepared for each stage ensures a holistic approach. Knowing when and how a product might be phased out or what might replace it helps manage transitions smoothly and maintain organizational equilibrium.

Launching a product—especially one designed for internal use—is not just about its inception into the organization; it's about foreseeing its journey, preparing the grounds for its arrival, ensuring its harmonious existence, and being ready for its eventual transformation or departure. This holistic vision ensures the product can deliver optimal value and align seamlessly with the evolving needs and goals of the organization.

Product Metrics and Performance Analysis

Measuring product performance and making data-driven decisions.

To effectively manage and improve internal software products, it is essential to track a set of specific metrics tailored to the needs and objectives of the organization. Product metrics and performance analysis are like the constant health check-up of the product, ensuring it's fit and robust and delivers optimal value in alignment with organizational needs and goals.

Let's imagine we have an internal tool designed to streamline procurement processes. Regular and meticulous analysis of how well this tool is performing can illuminate unseen crevices of improvements and optimizations. It's like having a regular check-up to see how well the heart of the operation is beating. Are the processes streamlined enough? Are there bottlenecks that need attention? Is the tool being used to its full potential, or are there features that remain untouched?

Measuring and analyzing product performance through key metrics provide tangible data on the product's health and value, enabling more informed and precise decisions to be made regarding its improvement and optimization. For example, if the tool's analysis reveals that a feature meant to fast-track approval processes is rarely used, it's a cue to delve deeper. Is the feature not user-friendly, or is it not adequately addressing the users' needs? Here, data-driven decisions aren't just reactionary; they are proactive measures that keep the product in its prime shape and in sync with strategic goals.

Continual feedback collection is the pulse that keeps the product alive and evolving. In the case of our procurement tool, regular inputs from users can reveal real-world challenges, experiences, and needs that might not be visible through just numerical data. Maybe the users find a feature cumbersome, or they might need additional functionalities to address emerging needs. This direct avenue of user insights becomes the compass, guiding refinements and enhancements to make the product more attuned to user needs and organizational objectives.

For internal software products, maintaining the balance between user satisfaction and alignment with organizational goals is a continuous journey. Regular measurements, thorough analysis, data-driven decisions, and constant user feedback are the navigational tools that ensure the product remains a valuable asset, adapting and evolving in harmony with the organizational ecosystem and contributing to the realization of strategic objectives.

Metric	Description	Why It's Needed	What to Watch Out For
User Engagement Metrics	These metrics include daily active users (DAU), monthly active users (MAU), and session length.	They provide insights into how actively users are interacting with the product, indicating product adoption and usage patterns.	Over-reliance on these metrics can lead to prioritizing features that drive engagement but not necessarily long-term value.
Operational Efficiency Gains	Metrics like time saved per task, reduction in manual errors, and process completion rate.	They help quantify the tangible benefits the product delivers to the organization, particularly in terms of operational efficiency.	Ensuring the accuracy of these measurements can be challenging; inaccurate tracking can lead to misleading conclusions.
User Satisfaction Scores	Gather through surveys, net promoter scores (NPS), or user-satisfaction ratings.	These scores assess how well the product meets the needs of its users and provide direct feedback from users about their satisfaction levels.	Scores can be influenced by external factors unrelated to product performance, such as personal interactions.
Real-time Dashboard	A tool that provides real-time insights into metrics like DAU, MAU, operational efficiency, and user satisfaction.	Enables Product Managers to monitor performance continuously and react quickly to any negative trends or opportunities for improvement.	Misinterpretation of real-time data can lead to hasty decisions without considering longer-term trends or data context.

Tales of the Product Manager

O nce upon a time, in the bustling world of SoftCorp, a vibrant team of developers, designers, and Product Managers named Team Accelerate was entrusted with creating innovative software to aid their internal users in their daily quests. The team, brimming with enthusiasm and eagerness, embarked on their journey with the belief that speed was the essence of success.

Deeming them mere formalities, Team Accelerate decided to leapfrog over the early steps of Ideation/Iteration and Market Research and dove straight into crafting the product strategy and roadmap. They believed that their intricate knowledge of internal systems and users would suffice, negating the need for extensive brainstorming or understanding user needs.

However, as fate would have it, their journey was fraught with unseen obstacles and continual failures. The software, born out of assumptions and haste, was a labyrinthine concoction of misaligned features and misunderstood needs. The internal users were left wandering in a maze of confusion, grappling with the inefficiencies and incongruities.

Amidst the chaos, a wise team member, Sage Analyst Sarah, realized the folly in their approach. She observed that they were blinded by skipping the initial steps, missing the beacon of key data and insights that would guide their path. Sarah voiced her realization to the team, highlighting the importance of each step in the Product Management Lifecycle.

With newfound clarity, Team Accelerate retraced their steps back to the beginning. They delved into Ideation/Iteration, brainstorming new ideas and identifying improvement opportunities with an open mind. They immersed themselves in Market Research, seeking to truly understand the needs and wants of their internal users.

With the collected wisdom, they redefined their Product Strategy and Roadmap, aligning it with the real needs and visions of the users. They meticulously crafted the Product Definition and Design, ensuring that every feature resonated with user needs and every function streamlined their tasks. The launch was planned with precision, and adoption strategies were crafted to ease the users into the new environment.

Finally, they embraced Product Metrics and Performance Analysis, measuring every aspect of the product performance and making data-driven decisions to continuously refine and enhance the software. The once chaotic journey transformed into a harmonious dance of alignment and clarity, the software becoming a beacon of efficiency and user satisfaction.

Team Accelerate learned the invaluable lesson that every step in the Product Management Lifecycle is a pillar supporting the structure of success, and skipping any would only lead to a shaky foundation and eventual collapse. They realized that patience, understanding, and adherence to the process were the true essences of success, making the journey as enlightening as the destination.

The internal users of SoftCorp rejoiced in the transformation, their daily quests now aided by a tool that truly understood and catered to their needs. Team Accelerate, with their spirits elevated and wisdom deepened, continued their journey in the cycle, always remembering the importance of each step and striving to create harmony and value in the world of SoftCorp.

The Product Management Lifecycle is a Cycle

The alignment of stakeholders, resources, and timelines is crucial to ensure smooth transitions through each Product Management Lifecycle (PML) phase. A skipped step has implications for every subsequent action, and because this is a cycle, it can even reverberate into the future of your delivery, showing up in unexpected ways (e.g., reduced trust from stakeholders).

During the Ideation/Iteration phase, aligning stakeholders fosters a unified vision and collective brainstorming. It's a harmonious convergence of ideas from various departments, such as IT, Finance, and Operations, to identify improvement opportunities and innovate. It's like assembling a diverse orchestra to create a symphonic blend of new product ideas. For example, finance stakeholders might highlight budget constraints or opportunities, while IT can shed light on technological feasibility and innovations. Ensuring everyone's on the same page at this stage sets the tone for the entire lifecycle, preventing misalignments down the line.

The Market Research phase is where aligning resources and understanding the wants and needs of the internal users is crucial. This is not about looking outward to understand the market but inward to comprehend your colleagues' needs, aspirations, and constraints. If the sales team desires a feature to streamline their processes but demands extensive resources, it's about finding the middle ground. It's like being the detective within your organization, gathering clues to piece together what your internal audience really needs and desires, and matching it with what can be feasibly delivered.

When developing a Product Strategy and Roadmap, aligning timelines is paramount. It's about plotting the journey ahead, ensuring that the vision and strategic direction are clear, and every milestone is realistically set. It is about having a meticulous game plan where every move is calculated, and every resource is allocated optimally to avoid overcommitment and ensure feasibility. For instance, planning the release of a feature to coincide with the end of a financial quarter might help in achieving organizational goals more effectively.

Clarity and precision are the lifelines in the Product Definition and Design phase. It's about translating the vision into tangible, actionable plans. It's drawing the blueprint, specifying features, functionalities, and aesthetics. At this stage, involving users to get their insights on the design can ensure the final product is user-friendly and meets their needs, like crafting a tailored suit that fits every user perfectly, avoiding costly alterations later on.

The Launch phase is the grand unveiling, where meticulous planning for adoption strategies is vital. It's about making the transition seamless for users and ensuring maximum value delivery. Preparation for post-launch support and ensuring continual user satisfaction is like the after-sales service, maintaining the product's performance and resolving any immediate concerns. For example, a smooth and well-communicated launch of a new HR tool can lead to quicker adoption and less resistance among employees.

Lastly, in Product Metrics and Performance Analysis, the alignment of all elements plays out in a symphony of data-driven decisions and refinements. It's continually measuring, analyzing, and refining, ensuring the product remains in harmony with user needs and organizational goals. It's like continually tuning a musical instrument, maintaining its optimal sound quality and adjusting it as needed. We identify where we need to focus next to ensure we remain "in tune."

Navigating through each phase with aligned stakeholders, optimized resources, and synchronized timelines is like conducting a symphony, where each note and each instrument plays in harmony to create a melodious masterpiece, an internal software product that resonates with the users and aligns with the organizational rhythm.

Points to Ponder

 How effectively do you navigate through each phase of the Product Management Lifecycle? Reflect on any phases where your process might be stronger or weaker.

 Are your stakeholders aligned at each stage of the product lifecycle? Consider how you manage communication and expectations throughout the lifecycle.

 How do you incorporate feedback and iterative improvements into your product management process? Think about whether your current approach allows for continuous improvement.

Gathering User Needs
and Prioritization

Understanding user needs is the bedrock upon which successful product management is built. For Product Managers, delving deep into these needs is not merely an operational necessity; it's a fundamental part of their role. It is about creating solutions that connect with users and finding the equilibrium between user needs, technological possibilities, and organizational goals. It is about discerning not just the articulated needs of the users but also uncovering the latent ones, ensuring that the product solves recognized problems and enhances user experience in ways users might not have envisioned.

In the realm of internal software development, this understanding is especially crucial. With users being internal stakeholders, the relationship between Product Managers and users is characterized by proximity and a shared organizational context. This closeness allows for a richer and more nuanced understanding of user needs, enabling the creation of solutions that are finely tuned to user needs and organizational objectives. However, it also necessitates a higher level of responsibility and responsiveness from Product Managers, as any misalignment or oversight can have immediate and palpable repercussions. In this dynamic, understanding user needs is not just about fulfilling a set of predefined needs; it's about continual engagement and adaptation, ensuring that the product evolves in tandem with the shifting landscape of user needs and organizational objectives.

Eliciting User Needs

Creating a meaningful dialogue between Product Managers and users is essential, as it fosters a deeper and more nuanced understanding of explicit and covert needs. This dialogue can be facilitated through various techniques tailored to the organizational context and the specific nuances of the user base.

Conducting one-on-one interviews, for instance, can offer an in-depth exploration of individual preferences and needs, such as understanding the unique needs of different members of a marketing team for a new content-management system. This approach is particularly beneficial when dealing with complex, individualized needs but may not be as effective when gathering broad, generalized insights.

Surveys and questionnaires are another valuable tool, especially when seeking to understand the preferences and needs of a larger user base. They offer a scalable way to garner diverse insights, such as preferences on function-alities for a new HR tool. However, their effectiveness might be limited if the questions are not well-crafted or if the response rate is low.

Observing users interact with current tools can offer a window into implicit needs and practical workflow nuances, like seeing firsthand the challenges a sales team faces while interacting with a CRM tool. This method is incredibly insightful for understanding real-world use but is time-consuming and may not reflect the entirety of user needs.

Interactive workshops and brainstorming sessions can serve as a catalyst for users to voice their needs, expectations, and frustrations. A workshop with a finance team could reveal the essential features and workflow improvements needed in a budgeting tool. However, the success of such sessions heavily depends on the users' active participation and the conductor's facilitation skills.

Incorporating Design Thinking emphasizes empathy and focuses on user-centric solutions. It can lead to innovative solutions in, for example, a procurement software project by concentrating on user experience and design. However, it requires a willingness from participants to engage in creative and sometimes abstract thinking, which may not suit everyone.

Crafting use cases and user stories helps in visualizing user journeys and can uncover various needs and features, such as elucidating how different departments would interact with a new communication tool. This is essential for building a detailed picture of user interactions but can be time-consuming and may overlook some implicit needs.

Finally, maintaining continuous feedback loops is crucial for the iterative refinement of user needs. Regular feedback from users say, from a customer-support team about a ticketing tool, ensures continuous alignment with user needs. This technique is ongoing and should be embedded in the development process, but it requires a commitment to responsiveness and adaptation from the product team.

Balancing these techniques and adapting them to fit the specific context and user base ensures the developed product is deeply aligned with user needs and organizational goals, thus maximizing its relevance and value to its internal users.

Tales of the Product Manager

Once upon a time, in a bustling corporate landscape, there was a Product Manager named Sam. Sam was responsible for developing a new internal communications tool to enhance collaboration among the company's diverse teams. He was enthusiastic and had a vision, but in his zeal to create a revolutionary product, he unfortunately sidestepped the importance of stakeholder engagement.

Sam, with his team, created a sophisticated tool with an array of features he believed would revolutionize internal communication. Assuming his vision aligned perfectly with their needs, he rarely consulted with the actual users or key stakeholders during the development process. When the time came to unveil the new tool to the company, he was brimming with anticipation, confident that his brainchild would be met with widespread acclaim.

The reality was starkly different. The tool, with its myriad of unrequested features, was complicated and unintuitive. The employees, perplexed by the complicated interfaces and redundant features, were reluctant to adopt it. They found sticking to their old methods easier, almost instantly rendering Sam's sophisticated tool an unused relic.

The critical voices reached a crescendo when department heads, frustrated by the misalignment between the tool and their teams' actual needs, vehemently voiced their concerns. They questioned the value of a product developed in isolation without understanding the on-the-ground realities and actual needs of its intended users.

Sam, initially defensive, was eventually humbled by the cascade of critiques. He learned the hard way that vision, no matter how revolutionary, could not be a substitute for a grounded, collaborative understanding of user needs.

He realized that stakeholder engagement was not just a box to tick but a critical component in developing products that genuinely solve problems and add value.

Chastened, Sam decided to retrace his steps. He initiated open dialogues with the users and stakeholders, conducted workshops to understand their pain points, and encouraged continuous feedback. He learned to listen, adapt, and mold his vision according to the actual needs and expectations of the users. The journey was arduous, filled with iterations and revisions, but eventually, Sam and his team managed to reshape the tool into a solution that the organization embraced.

From then on, Sam never overlooked the importance of harmonizing his vision with his stakeholders' practical needs and insights. He learned that the essence of successful product management lay not just in innovation but in empathy, collaboration, and a relentless pursuit of user-centric value.

Prioritization

When it comes to prioritizing user needs, having a structured approach is pivotal. Once the needs have been clearly outlined and understood, it's essential to sift and sort through them, discerning which ones are crucial and which can be deferred.

The MoSCoW method is an excellent starting point (Agile Business, n.d.). It segments user needs into Must-haves, Should-haves, Could-haves, and Won't-haves, simplifying the categorization process. For example, when developing a document management system for internal use, a search functionality may be a Must-have, while a feature to preview documents might be a Should-have. This method is particularly useful when the project has clear and non-negotiable deadlines as it helps to focus on the most critical features first.

The Value vs. Effort Matrix is another invaluable tool, aiding Product Managers in weighing the benefits of a feature against the effort and resources needed to implement it (Clark, 2024). In the context of internal software, where budgets and timelines are often tight, leveraging this matrix can ensure that the developed features yield maximum value with the least resource strain. It is useful when there is a need to deliver quick wins or when resources are constrained, but it can sometimes oversimplify the complexities involved in developing a feature, so it should be used judiciously.

The Kano Model is another technique that helps understand customer preferences over time. It categorizes features into Basic Needs, Performance Needs,

Excitement Needs, and Needs, and Reverse Needs. For example, in developing internal financial software, a user-friendly interface might be a Basic Need, while an automated report generation feature might be an Excitement Need. This model is beneficial when customer satisfaction is a priority, but it might not be suitable when the focus is solely on functional needs or when dealing with a very constrained timeline or budget.

The Buy a Feature method is a collaborative prioritization technique where stakeholders are given a fixed amount of "money" to "buy" features they consider the most important (Toxboe, 2023). This method is suitable when there is a need for stakeholder engagement and consensus, but it may not be as effective when dealing with a very large number of features or when stakeholders have vastly different priorities.

Dynamic Value Curation is an innovative approach that applies Monte Carlo simulations to a broad spectrum of tangible and intangible benefits (*Journey to VMO*, n.d.). By revealing discounted cash flows often overlooked in traditional business cases, thereby providing a more nuanced Cost of Delay, it enables a more comprehensive assessment of the true economic value of diverse initiatives. This approach often empowers internal products to compete effectively with client-facing initiatives, ensuring a balanced and objective prioritization process.

Using these prioritization techniques, the Product Manager can create a well-defined roadmap attuned to the users' operational needs, ensuring that the developed software is valuable and relevant. For internal software, it is often the immediate and practical needs of the users that take precedence, and these methodologies can help in aligning the product development efforts accordingly.

Prioritizing well is crucial for aligning product development with business goals, no matter which method is used. It's essential to make sure that we put our time, people, and money where they make the most impact and drive the business forward. By prioritizing effectively, we can clearly outline our product roadmap, making it a practical representation of the business's objectives and ensuring that every feature we develop is meaningful and contributes to our goals.

For internal software development, getting the priorities right is the foundation for creating products that meet user needs and business objectives. It allows the organization to get the most value from its software, focusing on features and enhancements that improve operational efficiency and employee productivity. For example, prioritizing a feature that eliminates a manual, cumbersome process can help remove operational hurdles, allowing the team to focus on tasks that add more value, and supporting the achievement of business goals.

In essence, setting the right priorities ensures that product development is in sync with business goals and user needs, and it helps avoid wasted efforts on less impactful features, ensuring the final product truly reflects what the organization and users need.

It's important to remember that each prioritization technique has its strengths and limitations, and it's often beneficial to use a combination of these methods or to adapt them according to the specific context and constraints of the project. Additionally, the prioritization should not be a one-time activity but a continuous process, adapting to evolving needs and constraints as the project progresses.

There are many, many, many techniques for prioritization, each suitable for different scenarios. The following summary table contains those previously described with other common methods.

Technique	Description	When to Use	When Not to Use
MoSCoW Method	Categorizes user needs into Must-haves, Should-haves, Could-haves, and Won't-haves.	With clear deadlines and limited resources.	In very dynamic environments where user needs change frequently.
Kano Model	Classifies features based on customer satisfaction into five "Needs" categories.	In customer-focused products seeking to balance delight and necessity.	When there's limited data on customer preferences or urgent development timelines.
Value vs. Effort Matrix	Balances the benefit of a feature against the effort required to implement it.	For projects needing quick wins with resource constraints.	In complex projects where simple cost-benefit analysis is insufficient.
Buy a Feature	Stakeholders use limited "money" to "buy" features they most value.	When engaging stakeholders and aligning on priorities.	For large sets of features or when stakeholder consensus is not critical.
Weighted Scoring	Assigns scores to features based on various criteria to rank them.	When multiple objective criteria need to be considered.	In small or straightforward projects where effort outweighs benefits of detailed analysis.
Opportunity Scoring	Evaluates features based on potential market opportunity.	In market-driven products aiming for growth.	In well-established products with a fixed user base.
Cost of Delay	Quantifies the financial impact of delaying a feature's implementation.	When prioritizing features with significant revenue implications.	When all features have similar impacts on revenue.

RICE Scoring	Considers Reach, Impact, Confidence, and Effort to prioritize features.	In data-driven environments where these metrics can be estimated.	When data is insufficient to make informed estimates.
Story Mapping	Organizes user stories into a map to visualize dependencies and priorities.	In agile development environments to maintain user focus.	In non-agile settings or where user stories are not used.
Priority Poker	Uses a game-like format for team members to vote on feature priorities.	When there's team engagement and consensus in agile settings.	With remote teams or environments where live discussion is challenging.
Eisenhower Matrix	Categorizes tasks by urgency and importance.	For effective time management and immediate prioritization needs.	In long-term strategic decision making.
Impact/Urgency Matrix	Prioritizes tasks based on their urgency and impact on the business.	When needing to balance quick wins with important strategic initiatives.	In projects where all tasks are equally urgent or impactful.
Feature Buckets	Sorts features into categories such as current, near-term, and future.	Balancing various strategic objectives.	When product strategy is unclear or the market is undefined.
Customer Voting	Allows customers to vote on features they find most valuable.	In direct customer engagement and feedback-driven products.	In high-stakes features that require expert decision-making.
Prune the Product Tree	Visual tool where stakeholders place features on a tree to show preference and impact.	For interactive workshops to align team and stakeholder vision.	In environments where quick, decisive action is needed without lengthy discussion.

Buy-In and Negotiation

Getting everyone aligned is crucial to navigating internal software development successfully. When you're dealing with different, sometimes clashing, stakeholder needs, it's important to keep communication lines open. Every stakeholder's concern must be heard and addressed to reach a common, agreeable product vision.

When priorities clash, having open and mediated discussions is key to understanding the underlying needs and restrictions of each stakeholder.

Product Managers need to steer these conversations, ensuring that everyone understands each other's position and the overarching goals of the organization. This shared understanding can make finding common ground easier.

For example, if the IT team is pushing for high-level security measures that might affect the product's usability, a mediated discussion can help find a solution that addresses security concerns while maintaining a user-friendly design. Using clear examples and demonstrations during these discussions can clarify the impacts of each proposed solution and help find a balanced approach.

Sometimes, though, even the most well-facilitated discussions can't resolve differences, and it's necessary to escalate the issue to senior leadership. In such situations, it's important to frame the disagreement as a difference in approach to achieving common goals rather than as a conflict. Providing a clear summary of each position and its benefits and risks can help senior leaders make decisions that align with the overall organizational strategy.

In short, reconciling varied stakeholder interests involves clear communication, diplomacy, and a focus on shared goals. It's about finding common ground, compromising where necessary, and sometimes, taking disagreements to higher authorities to ensure the final product meets everyone's needs and aligns with organizational objectives. This approach is essential in internal software development, where balancing diverse functionalities is often necessary to deliver comprehensive and effective solutions.

Points to Ponder

 What methods do you use to gather and prioritize user needs? Reflect on whether these methods effectively capture the true needs of your users.

 How do you manage conflicting priorities among stakeholders? Consider your strategies for negotiation and consensus-building.

 Are your processes to gather user needs aligned with your overall product goals? Think about how you can ensure that the gathered user needs truly reflect your product's vision.

Navigating
Organizational Politics

Navigating the intricate web of organizational politics is a vital skill for Product Managers, especially those focusing on internal software delivery. The complex interplay of differing interests, power structures, and personal ambitions within an organization can significantly impact the trajectory and success of a product. For Product Managers, understanding these internal dynamics is critical to manoeuvring through potential obstacles and facilitating the smooth implementation of software solutions.

Understanding the landscape of internal power dynamics enables Product Managers to identify allies and influencers who can champion the product, aid in overcoming resistance, and secure necessary resources. It helps in framing communication and proposals in a way that aligns with the motivations and priorities of key stakeholders, thereby garnering support and mitigating conflicts. For instance, approaching stakeholders with a clear depiction of how the product aligns with their objectives and the overall organizational goals can help in gaining their buy-in.

To understand and navigate organizational politics, Product Managers can employ active listening to discern stakeholders' unspoken needs and concerns, foster open and transparent communication to build trust and rapport, and maintain a solution-oriented approach to address the underlying fears and reservations effectively. Regularly engaging in one-on-one discussions, maintaining an open-door policy, and being empathetic to stakeholders' perspectives and constraints can help build alliances and navigate the political landscape more effectively.

In essence, a nuanced understanding of organizational politics enables Product Managers to strategically position their product, anticipate resistance, and adapt their approach to suit the varying needs and priorities within the organization, ultimately contributing to the successful delivery and adoption of internal software solutions.

Be Your Own Advocate

Product Managers often have a need to advocate for resources and budget. Many organizations have an annual planning cycle where such things get approved. In that situation, Product Managers should craft a compelling narrative grounded in clear, quantifiable benefits and aligned with organizational objectives. It is fundamental to demonstrate a clear understanding of the business's goals and illustrate how the proposed product supports them. A well-structured business case, emphasizing the anticipated return on investment, reduced operational costs, and increased productivity, can substantiate the ask and resonate with decision-makers.

For internal software Product Managers, tailoring the conversation to the stakeholder's concerns and motivations is essential. Focusing on cost efficiency and return on investment is key when talking to finance. When discussing with IT, emphasizing the system's robustness, security, and supportability can be beneficial. Highlighting the user benefits and improved workflows will catch the attention of end-user representatives.

Product Managers should also be prepared to negotiate and prioritize features and phases of the project to secure initial buy-in, with a clear plan to scale and enhance as the product proves its value. Continuous, transparent communication about progress and successes will keep stakeholders informed and can facilitate additional support and resources as needed.

Maintaining flexibility and openness to feedback is also pivotal, as it helps adapt the approach and refine the ask based on the stakeholders' inputs and concerns. However, it's equally crucial to stay firm on the essential needs and to escalate appropriately when the proposed cuts or modifications risk the product's success and value delivery.

A strategic, informed, and adaptable approach, grounded in organizational goals and stakeholder concerns, is key when advocating for resources and budget for internal software products. The ability to articulate the value proposition effectively, coupled with negotiation skills and organizational savvy, will help Product Managers navigate the resource allocation landscape successfully.

Handling Pushback

Handling pushback and resistance is an inevitable aspect of a Product Manager's role, particularly when dealing with internal software products for multiple stakeholders who have varying needs and priorities. When a Product Manager encounters pushback and resistance, it's essential to approach the situation with a combination of empathy, clarity, and resilience. They should actively listen and strive to understand the concerns raised by stakeholders, peers, or team members, as getting to the root of objections is central to addressing them effectively. A demonstration of understanding and acknowledgement of these concerns, irrespective of whether there is an agreement, can help maintain a harmonious working relationship and foster a positive environment.

Product Managers should clearly articulate the rationale behind their plans, roadmaps, or budgets and present data and evidence to support their decisions. Open, transparent communication about the objectives and benefits of their approach can help alleviate concerns and clarify any misconceptions. When faced with resistance, it is beneficial to reiterate the alignment of the proposed plan with the organizational goals and illustrate how it serves the larger business strategy.

It's also pivotal to stay adaptable. Compromise and flexibility in adapting plans based on valid concerns and feedback can lead to more balanced and accepted outcomes. It's also important to hold ground firmly where necessary, especially when the pushback is based on personal agendas or is contrary to the overall organizational objectives.

Negotiation and constructive dialogue are the keys when differences arise. If consensus remains elusive despite best efforts, escalating the matter to higher management with a clear, rational exposition of the conflicting viewpoints and their implications might be necessary. Throughout these processes, maintaining a professional, respectful demeanor is critical, ensuring the focus remains on the organizational success rather than personal conflicts.

Points to Ponder

 How well do you understand the power dynamics within your organization? Reflect on how this understanding impacts your ability to manage internal products.

 Are you effectively advocating for your product within the organization? Consider how you could improve your influence and communication with key stakeholders.

 How do you handle resistance or pushback from stakeholders? Think about the strategies you use to navigate and resolve conflicts.

Vendor-SaaS or
Internally Built

When **working** with internal products, Product Managers often find themselves balancing between two primary categories: internally built applications and Vendor-SaaS applications. Navigating through each requires different sets of strategies, considerations, and approaches.

Internally built applications are bespoke solutions tailored to meet an organization's unique needs and nuances. They offer a high degree of customization, allowing the organization to address specific user needs that off-the-shelf products may not meet. With such customization, businesses gain control over every aspect of the application, from its features to its user interface, enabling an ideal alignment with organizational workflows and processes.

But the luxury of customization comes with its own set of challenges. Developing an application in-house can be resource-intensive, consuming substantial time, effort, and money. Additionally, the organization takes on full responsibility for the application's maintenance, updates, and troubleshooting, necessitating a dedicated team to manage these ongoing needs.

Conversely, Vendor-SaaS applications represent pre-built solutions offered by external providers. These applications are typically more cost-effective and can be implemented more quickly than in-house software development. Organizations can benefit from the vendor's expertise, regular updates, customer support, and maintenance services, reducing the burden on internal teams.

However, while Vendor-SaaS applications are convenient, they might not offer the same level of customization as internally built applications. There can be limitations in adapting them to an organization's specific needs and processes. Moreover, reliance on external vendors implies a loss of control over the application's development and maintenance cycles, which could pose challenges in the long term, especially if the vendor's product roadmap diverges from the organization's evolving needs.

In working with a Vendor-SaaS, an extensive set of considerations must be made when moving through the Product Management Lifecycle. While navigating the ideation and market research phases for Vendor-SaaS solutions, Product Managers should consider not only the needs of internal users but also the available products in the market that align with these needs. They must meticulously assess potential vendors, evaluating their products against the organization's needs, budget constraints, and strategic goals. This involves a deep dive into each potential solution's features, customization options, scalability, and integration capabilities.

During the product strategy and roadmap phase, Product Managers must work closely with vendors to understand their product roadmaps and ensure alignment with the organization's strategic goals. This includes clarifying the frequency and nature of updates, understanding the vendor's approach to incorporating customer feedback, and negotiating service-level agreements (SLAs) to ensure the organization's needs will be met promptly and effectively.

In the product definition and design phase, Product Managers emphasize configuring and customizing the vendor's solution to suit the organization's needs. This might involve liaising with vendors to modify features, interfaces, or workflows and ensuring that user training and onboarding materials are tailored to the customized implementation.

Preparation and support are crucial for launching vendor solutions. Product Managers must coordinate with vendors to schedule implementations, manage disruptions to normal operations, and ensure that users can access adequate support resources. They also need to work alongside internal teams and the vendor to resolve any post-launch issues swiftly and ensure the product is well-received by users.

When it comes to product metrics and performance analysis, the Product Manager will need to establish clear metrics and KPIs that reflect the value derived from the vendor's solution. This includes assessing user adoption, satisfaction, and the impact of the solution on organizational efficiency and productivity. Close collaboration with the vendor is essential to gain insights from data and analytics provided by their platforms. (We will talk more about KPIs later in the book.)

In essence, managing vendor solutions in the Product Management Lifecycle is a multifaceted responsibility, requiring Product Managers to serve as the linchpin between the vendor and the organization, ensuring alignment between the product's capabilities and the organization's needs, goals, and values. Balancing the benefits of vendor solutions with the inherent limitations and risks requires a nuanced approach, clear communication, and ongoing vigilance to ensure the sustained success of the product within the organization.

Using Lean-Agile Procurement to Determine Software Solutions

Lean-Agile Procurement (LAP) offers a dynamic approach for Product Managers facing the decision between internally built applications and Vendor-SaaS solutions (Kleiner, 2023). By integrating LAP principles, Product Managers can navigate this decision with greater agility, ensuring that the selected solution aligns optimally with both the immediate and strategic needs of the organization.

LAP enhances the decision-making process by promoting rapid evaluation cycles, which are crucial when time constraints demand swift actions. This agility allows Product Managers to assess various solutions quickly and make decisions that are responsive to the organization's changing needs.

One of the core advantages of LAP is its emphasis on aligning procurement activities with the organization's strategic goals. This is achieved through stakeholder involvement from multiple departments, ensuring that the chosen solution—whether Vendor-SaaS or internally developed—supports overarching business objectives and integrates smoothly with existing systems and workflows.

LAP shifts the focus from merely considering the upfront costs to evaluating each solution's overall value. This approach aids Product Managers in presenting a business case for internally-built solutions that, while potentially costlier initially, may offer superior customization, better alignment with specific organizational needs, or lower long-term costs due to reduced dependency on external vendors.

For Vendor-SaaS options, LAP facilitates a deeper collaborative process with potential vendors. This not only includes assessing the technical capabilities of the SaaS products but also involves evaluating the vendor's ability to support agile, iterative improvements and customization, which are needed to maintain the relevance of the software as organizational needs evolve.

In essence, Lean-Agile Procurement is a strategic enabler for Product Managers, providing a robust methodology for navigating the complexities of software procurement and development complexities. By embedding LAP principles into their operational strategies, Product Managers can ensure that their decisions are both agile and deeply aligned with the long-term strategic needs of their organizations, thereby maximizing value and ensuring sustained success.

Tales of the Product Manager

Mike is a seasoned Product Manager in a large retail organization, and he's responsible for overseeing the company's e-commerce platform. He collaborates with a renowned SaaS vendor, CloudSolve, for the management and enhancement of the platform. The e-commerce platform is crucial, facilitating seamless interactions between internal systems and external solutions, all operating in the cloud.

Mike starts by conducting intensive meetings with CloudSolve to understand their offering fully. He keenly investigates how CloudSolve's services can integrate with his organization's existing systems and products, emphasizing minimal disruption and maximum compatibility. He meticulously outlines the strategic objectives of his organization and discusses how the SaaS solution can help achieve them.

During his interactions with CloudSolve, Mike is mindful of the internal needs and external market trends. He draws a comprehensive product roadmap, highlighting the enhancements and integrations required for aligning the platform with the company's vision and market demands. His roadmap is a meticulous blend of his organization's aspirations and the capabilities of CloudSolve, outlined with precise timelines and milestones.

As part of CloudSolve's user feedback group, Mike is in a prime position to influence the development of features by providing insights and feedback directly from his organization's user base. He organizes regular feedback sessions with his internal teams, ensuring that their experiences, needs, and preferences are communicated to CloudSolve accurately and promptly. Mike finds that this approach not only improves the quality and relevance of CloudSolve's developments but also fosters a sense of co-ownership and collaboration between his organization and the SaaS provider.

The partnership becomes symbiotic. Mike provides invaluable user insights and functional requirements that help CloudSolve fine-tune its offerings, making them more market-relevant and user-friendly. Conversely, Mike benefits from the enhanced and customized solutions CloudSolve provides, enabling him to drive user satisfaction and operational efficiency within his organization.

Mike also works closely with his organization's IT and Compliance teams to ensure seamless and secure integration of CloudSolve's solutions with internal systems. He advocates for proactive communication and collaboration between all parties involved to promptly address any concerns or challenges.

As a result of his strategic collaboration with CloudSolve and meticulous management of the product roadmap, Mike succeeds in creating a robust and user-centric e-commerce platform. The platform not only meets the evolving needs of his organization and its users but also stands as a testament to the power of synergistic collaboration between Product Managers and SaaS providers in building successful products.

In conclusion, Mike's story illustrates how effective collaboration with SaaS vendors, a clear understanding of organizational goals, and active participation in user feedback groups can help Product Managers build successful product roadmaps and contribute significantly to their organization's success. His approach highlights the importance of mutual growth and innovation in partnerships between organizations and their SaaS providers.

Points to Ponder

 How do you decide between using Vendor-SaaS solutions or building internally? Reflect on the criteria you use for making this decision.

 What challenges have you faced in working with Vendor-SaaS providers? Consider how these challenges compare to those of internal development.

 Are your Vendor-SaaS and internal solutions aligned with your long-term product strategy? Consider how you can ensure these solutions meet your organization's evolving needs.

Roadmapping and
Iterative Development

I**n the product development journey**, mapping out a clear path and adhering to flexible yet structured development methodologies are indispensable. This chapter delves into the essence of embracing agile methodologies, illustrating how their principles of adaptability, continuous improvement, and customer satisfaction are pivotal in fostering a product environment conducive to change and evolution.

Roadmapping is integral to product planning and strategy, acting as the navigational chart guiding the product through its developmental journey. Crafting a roadmap that clicks with internal stakeholders is crucial, ensuring that the product's trajectory aligns with the expectations and needs of those it is intended to serve. By connecting stakeholders to the product's journey, a well-structured roadmap can be a powerful tool in building consensus, managing expectations, and fostering collective ownership.

The journey is rarely without its challenges. Scope creep and influx of feature requests are commonplace, and managing them effectively is critical to maintaining the product's integrity and focus. This chapter will provide insights and strategies for maintaining a balanced approach to incorporating new ideas while staying true to the product's core objectives and values.

Through exploring these facets of roadmapping and iterative development, this chapter aims to equip Product Managers with the knowledge and tools needed to effectively navigate the complex terrain of internal product development, ensuring the delivery of products that are valuable, relevant, and aligned with organizational goals.

Agility Principles Support Product Management

Adopting agile principles in developing internal products is fundamental to fostering an environment that is adaptive, responsive, and resilient to the rapidly changing needs of users. Agile methodologies prioritize flexibility and responsiveness, enabling product teams to continuously adapt to changes and deliver value. This approach is particularly effective in internal product development, where user needs and organizational objectives are constantly in flux.

For instance, a team working on an internal tool to streamline workflow management can iteratively release features, ensuring the tool is continually refined and adapted based on user feedback and changing organizational needs. This not only reduces the risks inherent in software delivery by allowing for incremental improvements but also ensures that the product remains aligned with the evolving goals of the organization.

Moreover, agile methodologies support a culture of experimentation and learning within the development process. They encourage teams to test new ideas rapidly, fostering an environment where innovation is integral. By implementing quick test cycles, teams can evaluate the effectiveness and relevance of features or modifications and make immediate adaptations.

Consider a product team devising a novel feature for an internal communications tool to enhance collaboration. Agile principles would facilitate the swift introduction and assessment of this feature, allowing for rapid feedback and enabling instant adaptations based on user responses. This methodology creates a framework for "safe failures," where any unsuccessful feature or adjustment is a small, controlled, and valuable opportunity for learning and improvement.

Such an approach to failure ensures that any missteps in the development process are immediately identified and rectified, preventing any long-term detrimental impact on the product or the user experience. These "safe failures" are vital as they uncover invaluable insights and potential areas for innovation and refinement.

Embracing agility in product-development processes allows for continuous innovation and improvement, shaping the product into a dynamic solution that evolves in tandem with user needs and organizational objectives. The constant iteration and learning from both successes and "safe failures" are crucial in ensuring the developed product meets current needs and adapts to the ever-evolving demands of internal users. The amalgamation of these agile principles ensures that the product remains relevant, user-centric, and aligned with the strategic goals of the organization, enhancing its value proposition in the long run.

Building a Roadmap

Building a product roadmap that is aligned with internal stakeholders' needs directs organizational efforts and resources effectively toward product development. A roadmap should clearly convey the planned features and enhancements and serve as a strategic document, clarifying the product's vision, direction, and progress.

Tailoring and effectively communicating the roadmap to various stakeholders is key, as each group has different interests and concerns. Technical teams often delve into feasibility and implementation, end-users focus on usability and functionality, and leadership looks at alignment with broader organizational goals and strategies.

When a thorough understanding of the product is necessary, using a narrative technique to tell its story and how it meets user needs and solves their problems is highly effective. This method provides context and coherence, making the roadmap relatable and impactful to varied stakeholders.

Alternatively, when stakeholders need a quick overview of the product's direction, visual roadmaps with clear diagrams or charts are more suitable, especially during initial and periodic updates where in-depth discussions aren't needed.

Prioritizing features on the roadmap is necessary, and tools like the Value vs. Effort Matrix and the MoSCoW method, which we've discussed before, help balance stakeholder needs, resource availability, and organizational objectives. In cases of divergent priorities and opinions, open discussions and, if necessary, escalation to senior leadership are essential to reconcile differences and build consensus.

Remember, the roadmap is a dynamic document continually refined based on feedback and changes in organizational objectives and user needs. Regular interactions with stakeholders and their feedback are crucial for ensuring the roadmap accurately reflects the product's journey and organizational aspirations. Consider these strategies to enhance roadmap flexibility:

Use a Rolling Roadmap Framework: Instead of static long-term plans, adopt a rolling roadmap that evolves at regular intervals—such as quarterly or bi-annually. This approach allows you to adjust your strategy based on the latest company priorities, technological advancements, and user feedback.

Maintain Stakeholder Communication: Establish a clear communication channel with all stakeholders, including regular roadmap reviews, to align expectations and gather feedback. Transparent communication helps mitigate resistance and builds consensus on the roadmap's direction.

Use Scenario Planning: Include scenarios that account for potential changes in the business environment, such as shifts in market demand or internal resource availability. Scenario planning helps stakeholders understand possible outcomes and prepares the team for swift adaptation.

Do Contingency Planning: Develop contingency plans for critical roadmap milestones. These plans should detail alternative courses of action if the initial plans are disrupted, ensuring that the product remains on track even when unexpected challenges arise.

By integrating these elements into your roadmap strategy, you can ensure that your product development process remains adaptive and aligned with current and future business needs. This flexible approach reduces the risk of setbacks and ensures the product continually evolves in sync with the organization's objectives.

To summarize, a well-communicated, adaptable, and resonant roadmap, clear prioritization, and effective stakeholder management form the foundation for realizing the product vision and strategy in internal software development. The techniques and approaches chosen should align with the context and the specific needs and preferences of the stakeholders, uniting every aspect of the organization in a cohesive direction.

Scope Creep or Feature Request

Managing scope creep and feature requests is a core challenge in product development, especially with internal products where stakeholders have direct access to the product team. With evolving business needs and continuous user feedback, the influx of new user needs and changes can threaten to derail a product's progress and stretch resources thin.

It's essential to distinguish between genuine feature requests that can add value and scope creep, which may divert resources without a corresponding benefit. Scope creep often arises due to ambiguous project objectives, inadequate stakeholder communication, or not setting clear boundaries from the outset.

A proactive approach to managing scope creep involves setting clear definitions for the product scope at the start. Regularly revisiting these definitions in stakeholder meetings can keep everyone aligned. When stakeholders propose alterations or additions, evaluate them based on their alignment with the product's core objectives and their potential ROI.

For instance, if an internal department requests a feature that serves only its unique needs but doesn't align with the broader goals of the software, it may be better to defer it. On the other hand, if a requested feature can enhance efficiency across multiple departments, it's worth considering.

Feature requests can offer invaluable insights into user needs and gaps in the current product. However, not all feature requests are equal.

Using techniques like the Kano Model can help. While Basic Needs are essential for the product's functionality, Excitement Needs can offer a competitive edge. Recognizing which category a feature request falls into can guide its prioritization.

Another method is the Feature Buckets technique, which divides requests into three categories: current, near-term, and future. Immediate needs that fit the product's strategic goals fall into the "current" bucket. Requests that align with the product's direction but aren't immediately urgent are "near-term," while features that are more speculative and need more validation are placed in the "future" bucket.

In environments where feedback is continuous and resources are limited, a simple "cost vs. benefit" analysis can often be the most direct. Estimating the development cost of a feature against its projected benefits can prioritize features that give the best value. The Dynamic Value Curation approach mentioned earlier can be particularly helpful in these situations.

In situations with conflicting opinions on feature requests, facilitating open discussions with stakeholders can be helpful. This dialogue ensures everyone's concerns are heard, and decisions are made transparently. If a consensus is hard to reach, having a decision framework or escalating to higher leadership may be necessary, as discussed previously.

In summary, managing scope creep and feature requests is about maintaining a clear vision of the product's objectives, understanding the value of each request, and making informed decisions. By setting clear boundaries, regularly engaging with stakeholders, and using appropriate prioritization techniques, Product Managers can navigate the complex terrain of internal software development while ensuring they deliver a product that truly serves the organization's needs.

Tales of the Product Manager

At Acme Corp., a well-intentioned coder named Jamie decided to add a quirky feature into a new application, not required by the project but surely, in Jamie's view, a fun addition. It was a hidden game, which a specific sequence of keystrokes could access. It became a sort of secret, a chuckle among the teams, a corporate inside joke. Teams began sneaking in unrequested features, or "Easter eggs," into their projects, cheekily waiting to see who would stumble upon them first.

While these secret features became a source of amusement and camaraderie among the teams, they also represented unapproved augmentations to the project's scope. Each seemingly innocent addition could disrupt the planned features and affect the project timeline, potentially leading to unforeseen consequences.

In this case, rather than leading to disastrous outcomes, these playful additions indirectly fueled a new corporate tradition—"Innovation Days." The management, recognizing the creativity brewing among the teams, decided to allot one week each quarter for them to code freely—to let their imaginations run wild without the strings of project limitations and deadlines.

Although Jamie's initial deviation was seemingly harmless and eventually led to a positive cultural shift, it also highlighted the potential risks inherent in scope creep, underscoring the importance of maintaining a balanced approach to project creativity and adherence to agreed-upon project scopes. The risk of playful or "innovative" additions potentially overshadowing or derailing the primary objectives of a project should always be mitigated and managed effectively.

Points to Ponder

 How does your roadmap reflect the strategic direction of your product? Reflect on how well it aligns with both short-term needs and long-term goals.

 What challenges have you faced with scope creep or feature requests? Consider how you manage these challenges while maintaining focus on core objectives.

 Are you effectively using iterative development to refine your product? Think about how you could improve how you gather feedback and make adjustments.

Usability
and Training

When developing internal software, Product Managers must ensure that usability and user training are at the forefront of the product lifecycle, as these elements are necessary for the successful adoption and use of the product within an organization. Tailoring user experience, creating effective onboarding and training processes, and embracing continuous feedback and iteration are interlinked components, each crucial to user-centric development and refinement of internal products. They're all about optimizing every interaction users have with the product, from the first contact to everyday use, ensuring that the product continually meets the organization's needs and adds value.

The connection between these components is clear; a carefully tailored user experience can significantly ease the onboarding and training processes, while continuous feedback ensures that the product evolves with user needs and preferences. This collaboration results in a product that is not only well-received initially but continues to adapt and improve, maintaining a conducive environment for ongoing user satisfaction and engagement. By addressing these interconnected domains, Product Managers can develop a comprehensive approach to internal product development, maximizing the overall impact and success of the product within the organization.

Tailoring User Experience

Product Managers should collaborate with UX Design teams from the get-go. For instance, while developing a new internal communications tool, users from different departments should be involved in early design conversations. This can ensure the product addresses the varying needs and challenges across departments. Best practices include utilizing user personas to create designs that cater to diverse user needs and conducting usability testing sessions regularly to refine designs based on real user feedback. The focus should be on creating interfaces and experiences that are intuitive and user-friendly, reducing the learning curve for new users.

The tailoring of user experiences is not a standalone process; it's intricately connected to the processes of onboarding and training. A well-tailored user experience simplifies the onboarding and training processes, reducing the time and resources required to acclimate users to the new system.

Creating Effective Onboarding and Training Processes

In conjunction with Change Management and L&D teams, Product Managers must develop clear and concise training materials. For example, while rolling out a new HR software tool, engaging the HR team early on in creating role-based training materials can help ensure that the training is tailored to the actual users of the system. The best practice is to have hands-on training sessions, supplemented by easy-to-access online resources like video tutorials and FAQs, to accommodate different learning preferences. Product Managers should also facilitate feedback sessions post-training to refine future training programs based on user experiences and needs.

Customized Onboarding for Diverse Internal Teams

Design training sessions tailored to the specific roles and workflows of different departments. For instance, the finance team might need comprehensive training on reporting features, whereas the marketing team might require insights into data analytics functionalities.

Develop e-learning platforms with interactive scenarios and problem-solving exercises specific to your company's operations. This not only helps in understanding the tool but also in applying it to daily tasks effectively.

Identify and train key personnel within each department who can act as "knowledge champions." These individuals can facilitate peer learning and provide first-hand support to their colleagues, which is often more approachable and effective.

Feedback-Driven Training Enhancements

Integrate continuous feedback mechanisms within the training modules to allow employees to express their learning experiences and difficulties in real time. Use this feedback to make iterative improvements to the training process, ensuring it remains relevant and effective.

Establish key performance indicators (KPIs) for training effectiveness, such as user completion rates, post-training performance improvements, and user satisfaction scores. Regularly review these metrics to identify areas for enhancement.

Keep the training content dynamic by regularly updating it to reflect the latest tool updates and changes. Schedule periodic refresher sessions to ensure long-term retention and proficiency.

Example:

Consider a scenario where the IT department at a large corporation introduces a new internal project-management tool. The Product Manager coordinates with IT to create segmented training modules that address the specific needs of Project Managers, team leads, and administrative staff. They utilize an interactive e-learning platform allowing users to navigate typical project setups and troubleshooting. Feedback is continuously collected through the platform and used to adjust the content, such as adding more in-depth tutorials on features that receive higher queries.

Incorporating Best Practices in Training

Incorporate multimedia elements like video guides and interactive simulations that reflect common internal scenarios, making the learning process more engaging and practical.

Implement gamification to motivate employees through rewards, badges, or leaderboards based on their training progress and quiz scores. This makes learning more engaging and fosters a competitive spirit that can accelerate completion rates.

By focusing on these tailored strategies, Product Managers can ensure the successful onboarding and continuous use of new tools within the organization. This approach improves the usability of internal products and aligns training efforts closely with the unique workflows and cultures of different teams, enhancing overall productivity and satisfaction.

Remember, the role of Product Managers in training and onboarding doesn't stop once the initial training sessions are complete. It's an ongoing responsibility to address evolving user needs and expectations, intertwined with gathering continuous feedback and iterating the product. And remember, when your co-workers aren't happy, you will hear it from them.

Continuous Feedback and Iteration

Sustaining a regular feedback loop with users is paramount. For example, if users of a newly developed project-management tool find a feature confusing or lacking, quick iterations based on this feedback can lead to enhanced user satisfaction and product adoption. The best practice is to incorporate feedback mechanisms within the product, such as in-app surveys or feedback forms, and maintain open communication channels like regular user forums or discussion groups. This allows Product Managers to proactively address concerns, clarify any misunderstandings, and prioritize enhancements that are most impactful to the users.

By intertwining user-experience tailoring, comprehensive training processes, and continuous feedback, Product Managers can ensure the development of products that not only meet the initial user needs but continue to evolve and adapt to the ever-changing needs of the organization. The integration of these elements can drive successful product adoption and ongoing value delivery within the organization.

Points to Ponder

 How user-friendly are your internal products? Reflect on the feedback you've received about usability and how it has influenced your product design.

 What training processes are in place for your internal products? Consider whether these processes are sufficient to ensure smooth adoption and effective use.

How do you continuously gather and incorporate user feed-back to improve usability? Think about how this feedback loop could be strengthened.

Communication and Change Management

In a world where software and user needs are constantly evolving, Product Managers must orchestrate effective communication and change-management strategies. This chapter dives into the nuances of maintaining clear and ongoing communication about product updates and changes, ensuring that stakeholders are well-informed and can adjust to new functionalities or alterations in product features. Product Managers also play a crucial role in facilitating change within the organization, acting as liaisons between the development team and the user base, ensuring that transitions are smooth and that users are supported throughout any alterations in the product landscape.

Effective Communication of Product Updates and Changes

Communication is foundational in managing internal products. When communicating product updates and changes, it's crucial to be clear and concise to avoid misunderstandings. Utilizing visual aids, such as diagrams or screenshots, can clarify complex concepts or intricate changes, aiding in better comprehension. For example, a visual guide detailing a new feature can quickly elucidate its functions and benefits, promoting faster adoption among users.

Regular updates are equally critical, as they keep the user community informed and manage expectations effectively. This regularity in communication fosters a sense of reliability among users, minimizing any potential unease or resistance regarding upcoming alterations to the product. Providing a schedule or a reliable cadence of communications about updates ensures that users are well-informed and can prepare for upcoming changes accordingly.

Interactive sessions like webinars or Q&A forums can be very beneficial for more substantial or impactful changes. These sessions allow users to clarify their doubts and understand the reasons behind the changes, thus fostering a supportive environment and mitigating resistance during the adaptation period. Direct interactions like these also build a sense of community and inclusivity among users, contributing to a more user-friendly product environment.

Feedback during these sessions is invaluable. It allows Product Managers to gauge the reception of the changes and make necessary adjustments quickly. Addressing concerns and queries in real time not only clears up confusion but also demonstrates responsiveness and a user-centric approach, which are critical in building user trust and satisfaction.

In essence, effective communication of product updates and changes is not about bombarding users with information but about delivering the right information in the right way, at the right time. It is about creating a dialogue, a two-way street that not only informs but also listens and responds, contributing to a more user-centric product environment.

The Role of Product Managers in Change-Management Initiatives

Product Managers are central in steering change-management initiatives, serving as the conduit between the development teams and the end-users. They need to understand both user needs and organizational objectives to ensure that product changes align well with both. This involves working closely with Change Management and Learning & Development teams to smooth the transition and mitigate disruptions, ensuring users are well-supported throughout the change.

Anticipating and addressing the impacts of product changes on user workflows is also essential. This means preparing resources like training materials and support documents that users can refer to during the transition. For example, creating a detailed user guide or FAQ document can alleviate user anxiety and facilitate the adoption of new features or modifications.

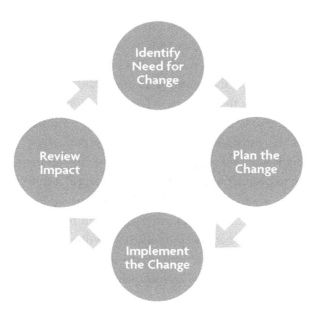

Devising change strategies requires extensive consultations with various stakeholders to enrich the change plan with diverse insights and to secure widespread support. The synergistic efforts of Product Managers, change agents, and other stakeholders ensure that changes are well-received and well-integrated into the users' workflows, leading to sustained user satisfaction and product success.

In addition, clear and open communication lines with users to gather their feedback and insights are vital. The integration of user perspectives makes the changes more user-friendly and acceptable. It demonstrates a commitment to user needs and preferences, fostering a positive and inclusive product culture.

The role of Product Managers in change management is multifaceted, involving close collaboration with various stakeholders, comprehensive support to users, and continuous refinement of change strategies to ensure smooth and successful product evolution.

Building a Feedback Loop with Internal Users

Establishing a robust feedback loop with internal users is crucial for the continuous refinement and enhancement of the product. It is fundamental for Product Managers to engage in regular interactions with users to grasp their experiences, expectations, and pain points accurately. Creating easy and accessible channels for feedback, like user forums or surveys, ensures that user voices are heard and considered in the product development process.

Addressing the feedback received is as important as collecting it. It builds user trust and fine-tunes the product to better align with user needs and preferences. Prioritizing and acting upon the feedback promptly demonstrates a commitment to user satisfaction and enhances the overall user experience.

Incorporating viable user suggestions and resolving reported issues contribute significantly to product optimization. For instance, if multiple users report a similar problem or suggest a specific enhancement, addressing it promptly resolves the issue and enhances user satisfaction and product reliability.

Such user-centric approaches in managing feedback rectify existing issues and aid in identifying areas for innovation and improvement. They ensure that the product meets the users' current needs and evolves to anticipate and address their future needs effectively.

An efficient feedback loop is not just about collecting user opinions but about creating a synergistic relationship between users and Product Managers. It's about making continuous improvements and innovations rooted in user needs and experiences, ensuring the product's relevancy and success in the long run.

Points to Ponder

 How effectively do you communicate product updates and changes to your users? Reflect on the channels and methods you use for communication.

 What role do you play in change-management initiatives within your organization? Consider how your involvement could be enhanced to ensure smoother transitions.

 How do you build a feedback loop with internal users to monitor the impact of changes? Think about how this loop could be more effectively utilized to drive continuous improvement.

Measuring
Success

I n the dynamic environment of product management, accurately measuring success is indispensable. The choice of what to measure is pivotal, and it can significantly influence a Product Manager's ability to make informed and impactful decisions. The improper alignment of key performance indicators (KPIs) and metrics can obscure issues, misdirect efforts, and ultimately lead to the failure of a product. Conversely, the right set of measurements can illuminate areas for improvement, guide effective resource allocation, and drive the continuous enhancement of the product. This chapter delves into the crucial aspects of measuring success in internal product management, exploring the selection and application of relevant KPIs and metrics, the implementation of effective tools and techniques for tracking product usage and user satisfaction, and the importance of leveraging collected data and feedback for the ongoing refinement and evolution of the product. Through the insights provided in this chapter, Product Managers will gain a comprehensive understanding of how to measure success accurately and leverage it to drive product excellence.

KPIs and Metrics

Determining the right KPIs and metrics is vital for gauging product success and areas for improvement. For internal products, a focus on usability and adoption rates is typically critical as they reflect the extent to which the employees find value in the product. To identify the right KPIs, Product Managers must deeply understand the organizational goals the software intends to meet and how the stakeholders interpret value.

To start, Product Managers should engage with stakeholders and users to discern their needs and expectations, and how they define success. This dialogue will reveal the priorities and desired outcomes the software should deliver, providing a foundation for building relevant KPIs. For instance, if a product's primary aim is to improve operational efficiency, metrics related to task completion times and user error rates may be pertinent.

Once the foundational understanding is established, Product Managers need to develop KPIs that are Specific, Measurable, Achievable, Relevant, and Time-bound (SMART). KPIs that adhere to these criteria ensure clarity, feasibility, and relevance, enabling teams to align their efforts effectively toward achieving the intended outcomes. For example, a SMART KPI for an internal communication tool could be to "Achieve a 25% reduction in email usage within the first quarter post-implementation," reflecting a clear, measurable, and time-bound goal.

In crafting KPIs, balancing leading and lagging indicators is crucial. Leading indicators can provide early insights into user behaviour and system performance, allowing for proactive adjustments, while lagging indicators offer a retrospective analysis of achieved results against the set objectives. Employing a mix of both allows Product Managers to monitor immediate impacts and long-term trends, facilitating comprehensive product evaluations.

Creating relevant KPIs lays the groundwork for effective product management, allowing the identification of success areas and opportunities for enhancement. However, having clear, relevant KPIs is just the starting point. Product Managers must use various tools and techniques to track these KPIs to continuously monitor usage and satisfaction, ensuring that the product meets the users' initial needs and continues to evolve based on ongoing feedback and changing user needs. The following section will delve deeper into the assortment of tools and methodologies available for tracking usage and gauging user satisfaction, providing insights into optimizing product value through continuous learning and adaptation.

KPIs profoundly influence initiative scope, primarily when the required metrics necessitate the creation of new features or adjustments to existing ones to facilitate measurement. While this is an integral part of developing a product that aligns with organizational goals and user needs, extending scope to include measurement tools can sometimes resemble scope creep, especially if it leads to substantial alterations in project deliverables and timelines. If the focus shifts predominantly toward constructing measurement systems rather than developing the actual product features, it can derail the project, causing delays and resource overallocation.

In such situations, it's crucial to maintain a balance. While it's essential to have the ability to measure the KPIs, the primary focus should remain on delivering value through the core features of the product. Product Managers must ensure that the development of measurement tools doesn't overshadow the fundamental objectives of the product. This balance requires clear communication about the importance of the measurement tools in aligning the product with the organizational goals and user needs, and careful prioritization to avoid unnecessary complexities and delays.

Additionally, Product Managers should be wary of "vanity metrics"—these are metrics that might look good on paper but do not contribute to the understanding of the core business objectives and don't help in making informed decisions. Vanity metrics are often deceptive and can lead teams away from their primary goals by presenting a superficial appearance of success. For example, a high number of app downloads may seem impressive but is meaningless if user engagement is low or if users abandon the app shortly after downloading it.

In another scenario, having a large number of features might make it seem as if a product is robust and versatile. Still, if users only interact with a fraction of them, the rest might just be inflating development costs without adding real value. In such cases, a more critical metric would be the usage rate of each feature, guiding Product Managers to invest in enhancing the features that are actually being used and valued by the users.

When establishing KPIs, the emphasis should be on selecting metrics that truly reflect the product's impact and value, avoiding those that offer a skewed or shallow view of success. Metrics should be actionable, providing insights that can guide decisions and strategies rather than merely serving as numerical embellishments to project updates. By doing so, Product Managers can ensure that the chosen KPIs genuinely enhance the product and align it more closely with user needs and organizational objectives.

Tales of the Product Manager

In a large corporation, the internal software development team led by a Product Manager, Mark, released a new feature intended to enhance employee productivity. The feature was a user interface deemed by the development team as sleek and modern and purported to increase user interaction.

During the quarterly business review, Mark, with his carefully prepared slides, confidently presented the impressive metrics to the senior leaders. The slides were filled with graphs indicating high login rates and interaction times, the chosen vanity metrics, projecting an image of widespread adoption and usage. Mark explained, "We've observed a substantial increase in user logins and interactions since introducing the new feature."

However, amidst the sea of approving nods, Steve, the leader of the primary users of the product, raised his hand. He was visibly unimpressed. "Mark, your numbers look great, but they don't address our real issues. My teams are frustrated; they're struggling with the basic functionalities of the software."

Taken aback, Mark tried to counter: "But the interaction times are through the roof—it shows engagement."

Steve retorted, "Mark, the increased interaction times you're so proud of are actually because the teams are struggling to navigate through the 'modern' interface. They're spending more time trying to figure out how to use it than actually using it! We don't need a stylish interface; we need a functional one. We need software that addresses our actual needs and makes our jobs easier, not more complicated."

Murmurs of agreement resounded around the room, the previously unseen frustrations now finding a voice.

This confrontation was a wake-up call for Mark and his team. They had fallen into the trap of vanity metrics, focusing on numbers that looked good on paper but failed to reflect the real-world usability and effectiveness of the product. The feature was not a success; instead, it was a source of frustration for the very users it was intended to help.

Mark and his team had to go back to the drawing board, this time focusing on the actual needs and experiences of the users, developing metrics that truly reflected the value and usability of the product. They learned the hard way that successful product management is not about creating features that look good in presentations but about delivering real, measurable value to the users. They focused on actionable metrics like user satisfaction and task completion rate and worked closely with Steve's team to modify the software to be more user-friendly and aligned with the users' needs, eventually restoring the users' faith in the product-development process.

Tools and Techniques

Mark's predicament underscores the urgent need for accurate and meaningful metrics, emphasizing the vital role of appropriate tools and techniques in correctly tracking user satisfaction and product usage. His situation serves as a reminder that measurements should genuinely represent user experience and the product's efficacy.

Product Managers should use usage data analytics to understand user interactions and behaviours within the software beyond traditional methods like surveys. This approach reveals the most used features and the user's journey through the software, and it points out where they might face issues or abandon the software. By examining usage data regularly, teams can pinpoint and address areas for improvement, enhancing user satisfaction and product value.

User Experience (UX) testing is another crucial technique. Observing users as they interact with the software can yield rich, qualitative insights. For instance, UX testing might disclose that a supposedly intuitive feature is confusing, offering opportunities for refinement that wouldn't be evident through quantitative methods alone.

Collecting feedback through surveys and UX testing enables a deeper understanding of user experiences and challenges, giving nuanced insights into the operational aspects of the software. These methods help determine if the software meets user needs and expectations and reveal areas that require refinement to improve user satisfaction.

Implementing Net Promoter Score (NPS) is also essential, clearly indicating user satisfaction by measuring the likelihood of users recommending the product to others. A high NPS suggests that the product meets user expectations, while a low score requires examining and improving potential issues.

For example, persistently low NPS scores necessitate immediate investigation. Understanding the reasons behind dissatisfaction allows Product Managers to address problems and adjust the product to align with user needs and preferences better.

Integrating diverse tools and techniques such as usage data analytics, UX testing, and NPS ensures a comprehensive understanding of user satisfaction and product usability. This combination of quantitative and qualitative insights allows Product Managers to make informed decisions and effectively refine the product to meet user needs and expectations.

The insights gained guide the continuous improvement of the product, enabling constant refinement based on user feedback and usage patterns. This approach ensures that the product development is user-focused, accurately meeting their needs and expectations.

The effective use of a variety of tools and techniques is crucial for accurately measuring and enhancing user satisfaction and product effectiveness. A balanced approach provides a complete perspective on user needs and experiences, facilitating the continuous evolution and improvement of the product based on real user feedback and behaviour.

Continual refinement and adaptation of the product based on these insights are crucial to ensure its relevance and value, avoiding the detrimental effects of focusing on misleading metrics, as Mark experienced.

Data and feedback offer a wealth of information about user behaviours, preferences, and experiences, acting as a compass that guides product development and refinement. Product Managers should regularly review the collected data, identify patterns and anomalies, and prioritize enhancements and adjustments accordingly. By continuously aligning the product with the evolving needs and expectations of the users, Product Managers can contribute to a more positive user experience and improved product performance.

For example, if user feedback and data indicate a feature is cumbersome and seldom used, Product Managers must respond promptly, seeking to understand the underlying issues and adjusting the feature to improve its usability and relevance. Conversely, highly used features may present opportunities for expansion or enhancement to further satisfy and delight users.

Continuous adaptation based on data and feedback also extends to introducing new features and innovations. Regular user feedback sessions, coupled with diligent examination of usage data, can reveal unmet needs and desires, providing a fertile ground for innovation. By maintaining an open, responsive approach to user insights, Product Managers can uncover valuable opportunities to introduce novel solutions and enhancements, elevating the product's value and user satisfaction.

The cycle of data analysis, implementation of insights, and subsequent feedback review is fundamental for continuous product evolution. Product Managers must remain vigilant and proactive in adapting products to meet user needs, leveraging precise and relevant metrics to refine and innovate continually. Mark's ordeal is a poignant reminder of the perils of neglecting this cycle, emphasizing the need to prioritize meaningful metrics and user-centric adaptations.

Points to Ponder

 What KPIs and metrics do you currently use to measure success? Reflect on whether these measures accurately capture the value your product delivers.

 How do you ensure that your success metrics are aligned with broader organizational goals? Consider how you could refine your metrics to better reflect these goals.

 What tools and techniques do you use for performance analysis? Think about whether your current tools are sufficient and how they might be improved.

Compliance and Ethical Considerations

Navigating the product-management landscape involves attention to compliance and ethical considerations, especially in the realm of internal product development. When creating products that colleagues will use, the implications of each decision magnify, echoing across various facets of the organization.

Ensuring Data Privacy and Security

Product Managers must place paramount importance on ensuring data privacy and security. Every feature and component must be scrutinized for its adherence to data-protection standards. For instance, imagine developing a new internal communication tool. If a Product Manager overlooks encrypting personal information, it may lead to substantial data breaches, profoundly affecting the employees and the organization. Therefore, incorporating robust security protocols and respecting user privacy is not optional but an integral element of responsible product development.

Privacy and security are not mere add-ons but are embedded within the product development lifecycle. A product riddled with security vulnerabilities can lead to the leakage of sensitive organizational data, thereby jeopardizing the integrity and reputation of the organization. By embedding security principles from the onset, Product Managers can protect sensitive data and uphold user trust.

Regular reviews and audits of security protocols and privacy policies are essential to maintaining high standards. Product Managers need to collaborate with IT security teams to keep abreast of evolving security threats, enforce stringent data-protection measures, mitigate risks, and ensure ongoing compliance with data protection regulations.

Illustrating the critical importance of data security is the well-publicized security breach at Equifax, one of the largest credit reporting agencies, which in 2017 suffered a severe cyberattack, exposing the sensitive information of 147 million people. The breach went beyond the mere loss of data; it broke the trust of millions and left them vulnerable to fraud and identity theft. Equifax had to agree to hefty fines and restitution, amounting to $700 million. It showcased the devastating results of neglecting security vulnerabilities and served as a reminder of the need for steadfast data-protection measures and frequent security assessments to promptly address potential vulnerabilities.

This incident underlines the importance of not just identifying but swiftly acting on security vulnerabilities and of maintaining robust data-protection standards. The Equifax breach exemplifies the destructive consequences of inadequate security measures and highlights the importance of instilling a culture of security awareness within organizations.

Compliance with Regulations and Standards

Beyond data security and privacy, compliance with regulations and standards is equally critical. Product Managers must be well-acquainted with the organization's policies and ensure that every aspect of the product aligns with them. For example, if an organization has a stringent policy against storing certain data types, violating this norm can lead to serious consequences.

Being well-versed in internal regulations ensures that the product does not inadvertently violate organizational norms or industry standards. Regular liaisons with the legal and compliance teams are crucial for staying informed about any updates to internal policies or regulations, enabling proactive adjustments to the product to maintain alignment with organizational standards.

In a scenario where the organization operates in a highly regulated industry, the lack of adherence to internal and external regulations can lead to legal repercussions and tarnish the organization's reputation. The endeavour is not to merely fulfill compliance needs but to exceed them, fostering a culture of responsibility and ethical conduct.

In 2016, Wells Fargo became the centre of a major scandal involving the creation of unauthorized accounts. Under immense pressure to meet sales targets, employees had opened millions of unauthorized bank and credit card accounts without customer knowledge or consent, leading to many fees and charges. This situation was not only an enormous ethical lapse but also a significant breach of compliance with federal banking regulations.

The aftermath of this scandal was devastating for Wells Fargo. It led to a fine of $185 million, with a $100 million penalty going to the Consumer Financial Protection Bureau (CFPB), marking the largest fine ever levied by the bureau at that time. The incident also resulted in severe reputational damage, leading to a loss of trust among customers and stakeholders.

For Product Managers operating in such environments, this incident serves as a poignant reminder of the importance of strict adherence to compliance standards and ethical norms. Any product, service, or feature developed should undergo rigorous compliance checks to ensure adherence to all applicable regulations, especially in sectors like banking, where regulatory frameworks are stringent.

The lesson derived from the Wells Fargo incident emphasizes the vital need for a robust compliance framework within product management processes. Adherence to federal and internal regulations must be an integral part of the product development lifecycle. Product Managers should work closely with compliance and legal teams to ensure every aspect of the product is in line with the applicable legal standards and ethical norms, thereby safeguarding the organization from legal repercussions and maintaining the trust and credibility of the product among users and stakeholders.

This integration of compliance from the inception of the product development process is not merely a protective measure but contributes substantially to the overall integrity and reliability of the product, reinforcing trust and ensuring the longevity and success of the product in the competitive market landscape.

Expanding Compliance and Security Measures in Regulated Industries

For Product Managers, compliance and security are not just regulatory obligations but the cornerstone of ethical product development. Managing software products that colleagues rely on demands a vigilant approach. Every enhancement or modification can echo across the entire organization, magnifying the implications of each decision.

As a Product Manager, it is essential to possess a deep understanding of the regulatory requirements that impact your specific industry. Whether it's GDPR in data protection, HIPAA in health care, or SOX in the financial sector, knowledge of these laws is crucial. This familiarity ensures that the software continually meets legal standards, thereby protecting the organization from severe penalties for non-compliance.

Implementing a robust compliance framework is key. This framework should outline how internal products are managed from their inception through development to deployment and operational use, integrating compliance checks at every stage. Regular compliance audits and risk assessments become part of the product lifecycle, designed to detect and mitigate potential violations early in the process. Such proactive measures safeguard the organization and reinforce the trust that users place in the system.

Security measures, too, must be tailored to meet specific industry risks. Whether it involves encryption, access controls, or secure coding practices, these security measures must address the unique threats faced by your sector. Collaboration with IT security to stay abreast of emerging threats is crucial, ensuring your internal software remains secure against evolving risks.

Training and awareness are equally important. Conducting regular training sessions for all teams involved in developing and using the software is crucial. These sessions should cover the regulatory standards and security practices relevant to your industry to ensure that every employee understands their role in maintaining compliance and security.

Clear documentation and reporting mechanisms are essential components of a thorough compliance strategy. They facilitate compliance verification during audits and enhance transparency with regulatory bodies by clearly outlining the measures in place to protect data and ensure compliance.

Leveraging technology that aids in compliance management can provide significant advantages. Automated tools that monitor compliance and alert managers to regulatory changes can help ensure that internal software continuously meets legal standards without requiring constant manual oversight.

By proactively managing these aspects, Product Managers safeguard their organizations against legal and security risks and build trust with users by demonstrating a commitment to ethical management and operational excellence.

The well-publicized security breach at Equifax starkly illustrated the need for such vigilance. This breach exposed the sensitive information of millions and highlighted the devastating results of neglecting security vulnerabilities. It served as a grim reminder of the need for stringent security measures and frequent assessments to promptly address potential vulnerabilities.

In essence, the role of a Product Manager transcends mere compliance; it is fundamentally about fostering a culture of responsibility and ethical conduct. This commitment to ethical management enhances the reliability and success of internal software products and supports the organization's overall integrity.

Ethical Considerations in Decision-Making

Beyond compliance and security, ethical considerations in decision-making stand as the backbone of product management. Every decision made should be weighed against its ethical implications. It might seem expedient to overlook minor ethical considerations for quicker results, but the long-term ramifications of such decisions can be detrimental to the organization's credibility and moral standing.

Product Managers need to consider the potential impact of their decisions on various stakeholders, ensuring fairness and avoiding harm. An ethically designed product not only abides by the principles of honesty and integrity but also respects the rights and dignity of its users. If, for instance, a feature can potentially be used to marginalize or discriminate against certain user groups, it is the Product Manager's ethical responsibility to reconsider its implementation.

Sometimes, ethical considerations may necessitate difficult trade-offs, requiring Product Managers to prioritize values over profits or convenience. Striking the right balance is crucial, as any compromise on ethical grounds can have lasting negative effects on user trust and organizational culture.

Product Managers should foster an environment where ethical considerations are openly discussed and addressed, facilitating collective moral growth and fortifying the organization's ethical foundation. By remaining steadfast in ethical considerations, Product Managers uphold the moral integrity of the products and contribute to building a more equitable and conscientious organizational culture.

The intertwining threads of data privacy, compliance, and ethical decision-making weave the fabric of responsible and effective product management. Product Managers stand as the guardians of these principles, ensuring that every product meets organizational needs while upholding the highest standards of integrity, security, and ethical conduct. Balancing these considerations is not mere compliance; it's a commitment to fostering a culture of responsibility and moral rectitude within the organization.

Points to Ponder

 How do you ensure that your internal products comply with relevant regulations and standards? Reflect on the processes you have in place for maintaining compliance.

 What steps do you take to protect data privacy and security in your products? Consider whether your current measures are adequate and how they could be strengthened.

 How do you balance innovation with the need for compliance? Think about the challenges you face in maintaining this balance and how you can address them.

Continuous Improvement: Nurturing Innovation and Adaptability

At the heart of any successful product or organization lies the philosophy of continuous improvement. It's a transformative journey involving meticulous refinement of products and processes and, most importantly, the organizational culture. Think of this journey as a symphony, where every innovative idea and every incremental enhancement resonates harmoniously, propelling organizational growth and product evolution.

To genuinely cultivate a culture of continuous improvement, it's imperative to embed an experimentation and learning-oriented mindset throughout the organization. The revered automobile manufacturer Toyota stands as a beacon in this realm with its "Kaizen" philosophy. By focusing on continuous improvement and actively involving all employees in suggesting small, incremental changes, Toyota managed not only to refine its production processes but also galvanized its workforce into a unit that always seeks improvement. This is a classic case of organizational culture symbiotically influencing product and process enhancement.

Yet, the spirit of continuous improvement isn't just about processes; it's also about innovation. Events like Hackathons or Innovation Days can serve as catalysts. Innovation should be a continuous pursuit within the product management team, deeply integrated into the organizational culture. Here are practical strategies to nurture innovation:

- Structured Innovation Programs: Implement programs that allow employees to propose and develop new ideas. These could take the form of innovation challenges, where employees form teams to solve specific problems or propose enhancements to existing products.

- Hack Days: Organize regular events, such as quarterly hack days, where employees can work on any project that interests them. These events encourage creativity and often lead to viable product improvements or new product ideas.

- Cross-Functional Collaboration: Encourage team members to collaborate with different departments. This exposure can spark new ideas and approaches, leveraging diverse perspectives and expertise.

- Rewarding Innovation: Establish a reward system that recognizes and incentivizes innovative ideas and successful implementations. Recognition can range from financial bonuses to public acknowledgment in company meetings.

- Learning from Failure: Create an environment where failure is seen as a stepping stone to innovation. Encourage teams to share what didn't work and why, fostering a learning culture that improves future projects.

By embedding these practices into your team's operations, you can ensure that innovation is not a one-time event but a continuous, value-driving process. This dynamic approach keeps your products at the cutting edge and aligns them more closely with evolving user needs and business goals.

But fostering a culture of continuous improvement isn't just about grand strategies or structured events. The onus is on organizational leaders, especially Product Managers, to exemplify behaviours that resonate with an adaptive and learning mindset. Taking a page from the leadership playbook of Satya Nadella, CEO of Microsoft, one realizes the transformative power of leadership in shaping cultural attitudes. Nadella championed the mantra of "Learn it all" instead of "Know it all," stressing the value of constant learning over merely resting on existing knowledge. His emphasis on adaptability over steadfastness has since become a guiding philosophy for many aspiring leaders.

Emphasizing the need to stay close to users, there's a potent tool in the form of user-shadowing. Companies like IDEO have long championed user-centric design thinking, wherein teams actively observe users in their native environments to fathom their needs and preferences. This direct insight ensures that the resulting products are technologically sound and empathetically crafted to align closely with user expectations.

While embracing innovation, it's essential to remain grounded in ethical considerations. Continuous improvement, after all, isn't just about relentless forward motion; it's also about ensuring the journey upholds the highest standards of integrity and compliance. As we've seen with incidents like the data-security lapse at Equifax, even a single oversight can have catastrophic implications regarding financial penalties and tarnished reputation.

For Product Managers and organizations at large, continuous improvement is a holistic ethos. It's not merely about refining products or processes. Instead, it's a philosophy that interweaves innovation, behavioural excellence, user-centricity, and ethical adherence to ensure both product and organizational success.

Points to Ponder

 How do you foster a culture of continuous improvement within your product team? Reflect on the practices or tools you use to encourage ongoing innovation.

 What barriers to innovation have you encountered? Consider how you've addressed these challenges and what more could be done to remove obstacles.

 How adaptable is your current product development process? Think about how well your process accommodates technological changes, market conditions, or user needs.

The Future of Product Management

In the evolving landscape of product management, the acceleration of technological innovation is reshaping roles and expectations. As we look to the future, the domain is set to experience a convergence of cutting-edge technologies, user-centric designs, and innovative practices, altering how Product Managers operate and deliver value within organizations.

Predictions and trends for the evolving field suggest that Artificial Intelligence (AI) and machine learning will continue to gain prominence, leading to more intelligent and informed product decisions. Integrating these technologies will allow for enhanced user experiences and smarter, more efficient workflows. Automation and advanced analytics will become indispensable tools for Product Managers, empowering them to optimize processes and base their strategies and decisions on accurate, real-time data.

In this dynamic environment, there is an increasing emphasis on understanding and prioritizing user needs and behaviours. This shift necessitates creating more personalized, intuitive, and user-friendly internal tools, thereby promoting higher levels of satisfaction and productivity among users. The focus on user-centric design will likely intensify, driving Product Managers to explore and implement solutions that align closely with user preferences and needs.

Acquiring a diverse and refined skill set will be crucial for the next generation of Product Managers. A deep comprehension of technology, strategic insight, and effective communication skills will be the cornerstones of successful product management. Collaborating across different departments and synthesizing diverse sets of information will be more critical than ever, especially as internal products become increasingly sophisticated and interconnected.

Adaptability and resilience will be the hallmarks of Product Managers in the future. The rapid pace of technological advancements and changing organizational needs will require them to be flexible and forward-thinking. A continuous learning mindset and a proactive approach to acquiring new knowledge and skills will differentiate successful Product Managers in this ever-evolving landscape.

Embracing innovations and the advent of emerging technologies such as blockchain, augmented reality, and the Internet of Things (IoT) is essential. These technologies promise to revolutionize internal products by enhancing security, enriching user interaction, and improving connectivity. The exploration and incorporation of these innovations will ensure that organizations remain competitive and future-ready, enabling them to pioneer novel solutions and functionalities in their internal products.

The integration of these technologies is not without its challenges. It necessitates a culture of curiosity, experimentation, and willingness to venture into the unknown. Product Managers must lead in fostering this culture within their organizations, inspiring teams to explore uncharted territories and implement groundbreaking solutions.

Product Managers must also emphasize and cultivate a culture of continuous learning and improvement to prepare their teams and organizations for the future. Keeping abreast of the latest trends, technologies, and practices in the field is imperative for staying ahead of the curve and meeting the evolving needs of users and organizations.

As we reflect on the future of internal product management, it is clear that the field is on the brink of exciting transformations. The amalgamation of innovative technologies, user-centric approaches, and advanced skills will reshape the domain, offering unprecedented opportunities for growth and development. By staying informed, embracing new possibilities, and continuously evolving, Product Managers can successfully navigate this transformative journey, significantly enhancing organizational success and user satisfaction in the process.

In conclusion, the journey ahead for product management is thrilling and filled with opportunities and challenges alike. The ability to foresee trends, adapt to new realities, and embrace innovations will determine the trajectory of

Product Managers and the organizations they serve. The synergy of foresight, adaptability, and innovation will be the catalyst propelling internal product management into a future marked by accomplishment and progress.

Points to Ponder

 How do you see the role of internal product management evolving in your organization? Reflect on how you can prepare for future trends and challenges.

 What emerging trends in product management are you most excited about? Consider how you can incorporate these trends into your current practices.

 How are you planning for the long-term success of your internal products? Think about the strategies you have in place to ensure they continue to meet the evolving needs of your organization.

Conclusion and Key Takeaways

In this exploration of internal product management, we've delved deeply into the nuances, methodologies, and strategies pivotal to curating efficient, user-centric software that is conducive to organizational objectives.

Agile Methodologies and Iterative Development

We opened our discussions focusing on the vital role of agile methodologies, highlighting their indispensability in facilitating flexibility and fostering a customer-oriented approach. These are crucial in continual product refinement and are the linchpin for ensuring the end product is precisely attuned to user needs and organizational goals.

Roadmapping and Stakeholder Alignment

The creation of succinct, coherent product roadmaps was underscored as being instrumental. It aligns stakeholders and manages scope efficiently, preventing potential derailments that can arise from misalignments and misunderstandings.

Usability and Training

A major emphasis was placed on the critical nature of effective user experience and the provision of streamlined onboarding and training processes. The collaboration between various domains within an organization is pivotal to realizing products that are user-friendly and leveraged to their fullest potential.

Communication, Change Management, and Feedback Loop

We discussed the intrinsic role of Product Managers in facilitating communication and managing change, concentrating on the importance of establishing robust feedback loops and ensuring product evolution is in tandem with user needs and organizational aspirations.

Measuring Success through Meaningful Metrics

Measuring success appropriately was another focal point. We explored the imperative need for choosing relevant KPIs and the risks associated with vanity metrics, which can be misleading and detrimental to product development objectives.

Ethical, Compliance, and Data Security Considerations

The importance of adherence to ethical standards and compliance was another key takeaway. Emphasis was laid on the absolute necessity to uphold data privacy and security norms to mitigate against potential legal ramifications and reputational damage.

Continuous Improvement and Organizational Innovation Culture

The essential nature of cultivating an environment that promotes continuous improvement and innovation was explored. Establishing such a culture is crucial for sustaining long-term organizational growth and success.

Looking Ahead—The Evolving Landscape

Lastly, we ventured into the future of internal product management. We talked about emerging trends, the competencies that will be required of the next generation of Product Managers, and the significance of embracing innovations and staying abreast of emerging technologies.

Wrapping Up

This guide is a practical compendium for internal Product Managers, encapsulating actionable insights, best practices, and real-world strategies for developing user-centric, efficient internal software. By leveraging the principles and strategies outlined herein, Product Managers will be well-positioned to deliver significant value to their organizations, ensuring the creation of products aligned with user needs and organizational objectives, driving user satisfaction and organizational success.

Tales of the Product Manager

Once upon a time in a forward-thinking tech enterprise, Jordan, a seasoned Product Manager, embarked on the journey to spearhead the evolution of an outdated internal communication system. The mission was to remove existing bottlenecks and fabricate a streamlined communication eco-system within the organization.

Jordan began by diving deep into conversations with various teams, striving to understand the nuanced needs and pains of the current system. With every conversation, whether with IT specialists, user representatives, or department heads, Jordan was piecing together a mosaic of user needs and perspectives. They used tools like MoSCoW to prioritize the work, ensuring the emerging user-centric roadmap was detailed and tailored to solve prominent pain points.

Jordan integrated agile methodologies into the development process, aiming for an adaptive and iterative evolution of the product. They organized regular review sessions, where stakeholders could offer insights and suggestions based on the sprint progress, ensuring the product was always on the right trajectory. Jordan utilized A/B testing and surveys during the development phase, collaborating with UX designers to refine the interface based on real user feed-back, placing paramount importance on creating an intuitive user experience.

To facilitate the smooth adoption of the new system, Jordan teamed up with Learning & Development and Change Management teams to devise comprehensive training and onboarding plans. Throughout the development cycle, they maintained transparent and continuous communication with internal customers, managing changes, addressing concerns, and integrating feedback to enhance the product.

A challenge arose when one team pressed for immediate implementation of a feature they found critical. However, catering to this urgent request would impact the delivery timeline set for another team. Jordan navigated this intri-cacy, managing the timeline and maintaining the overall vision and fairness in prioritization.

To track the product's impact and success, Jordan was meticulous in setting and analyzing KPIs, avoiding the pitfall of misleading vanity metrics. They implemented various tools and techniques, such as usage analytics and satisfaction surveys, to garner user feedback and pinpoint areas for improvement, ensuring the product was always in a state of refinement.

In their journey, Jordan was steadfast in upholding data privacy and compliance with internal regulations, a step crucial to maintaining user trust and product integrity. They also carefully integrated ethical considerations into every decision-making process throughout the product lifecycle.

In the post-launch phase, Jordan initiated innovation days and encouraged the team to explore creative enhancements and solutions, fostering a culture of continuous improvement and innovation. The launch was not the end; Jordan used the feedback and experiences from this cycle to refine strategies for future projects, embodying a spirit of constant learning and evolution.

Jordan's journey is a testament to the transformative power of adept product management in crafting solutions that are efficient and user-friendly and in sync with the organization's needs and values. Through their unwavering dedication, continuous learning, and meticulous approach, Jordan revolutionized the internal communication dynamics of their organization, setting a benchmark in value-driven, internal product management.

Points to Ponder

 What are the most significant lessons you've learned from managing internal products? Reflect on how these lessons have shaped your approach to product management.

 How can you apply the key takeaways from this book to your current projects? Consider specific actions you can take to implement these insights.

 What steps will you take to continue improving your internal product management skills? Think about the resources or learning opportunities you can pursue.

Appendix

Prioritization Methods

MoSCoW

MoSCoW (Must-have, Should-have, Could-have, Won't-have) is a prioritization technique that helps identify and categorize backlog items based on their importance and urgency. It enables the Product Manager and their team to distinguish between critical must-have items and less essential ones, allowing for better focus and decision-making.

Step 1. Identify Backlog Items:

1. Gather all the items in your backlog that need to be prioritized.

2. These items can include user stories, features, enhancements, or any work that needs to be completed.

Step 2. Define MoSCoW Categories:

1. Establish the four MoSCoW categories: Must-have, Should-have, Could-have, and Won't-have.

2. Ensure the team has a shared understanding of what each category represents.

3. Must-have: Items that are essential and critical for the product's success. They are mandatory and must be completed within a specific time frame.

4. Should-have: Items that are important but not critical. They provide value and should be addressed but have some flexibility in terms of timing.

5. Could-have: Items that are desirable but not necessary for the current release or iteration. They can be postponed or dropped if time and resources become limited.

6. Won't-have: Items that are explicitly excluded or not considered for the current project or release. They are deliberately deprioritized and not planned for implementation.

Step 3. Categorize Backlog Items:

1. Review each backlog item and categorize it according to the MoSCoW categories.

2. Consider factors such as business value, business needs, dependencies, risks, and any other relevant criteria to determine the appropriate category for each item.

3. Use discussions with the team and stakeholders to reach consensus on the categorization.

Step 4. Order the Priorities:

1. Within each MoSCoW category, establish a relative order of priority.

2. For example, within the Must-have category, identify the most critical items that need to be addressed first, followed by the ones of lesser importance.

3. Repeat this process for the Should-have and Could-have categories, ensuring that the highest-priority items come first.

Step 5. Communicate and Validate:

1. Share the prioritized backlog with the team, stakeholders, and any relevant parties.

2. Communicate the rationale behind the prioritization and seek feedback to ensure alignment and understanding.

3. Validate the prioritization with the team to ensure it is feasible and achievable within the given constraints.

Step 6. Continuously Review and Adapt:

1. Backlog prioritization is an ongoing process and should be revisited regularly as new information, feedback, or user needs emerge.

2. Continuously review and update the priorities based on changing circumstances, business feedback, market conditions, and project goals.

WSJF

WSJF (Weighted Shortest Job First) is a prioritization technique commonly used to prioritize backlog items based on their value, size, and urgency. It helps maximize value delivery by considering the cost of delay and the size of the work. The technique has the team assign a numerical value to each backlog item based on its business value, time criticality, risk reduction, and job size. It helps the team make informed decisions about which items to work on first by considering both the value and the cost of delay associated with each item.

Step 1. Define WSJF Components:

1. Identify and define the components of WSJF:

2. Business Value (BV): The perceived value or benefit of a backlog item to the business or user.

3. Time Criticality (TC): The urgency or importance of the backlog item based on market conditions, business needs, or business goals.

4. Risk Reduction Opportunity (RR): The potential risk reduction or mitigation that can be achieved by addressing the backlog item.

5. Job Size (JS): The relative effort, complexity, or size of the work required to complete the backlog item.

Step 2. Assign Numerical Values:

1. Assign numerical values to each component for every backlog item. The specific values can be based on a scale of your choice, such as 1 to 10 or Fibonacci sequence.

2. For example, you might assign a Business Value of 5, Time Criticality of 8, Risk Reduction Opportunity of 3, and Job Size of 13 to a particular backlog item.

Step 3. Calculate WSJF Score:

1. Calculate the WSJF score for each backlog item by dividing the sum of Business Value, Time Criticality, and Risk Reduction Opportunity by the Job Size. WSJF Score = (BV + TC + RR) / JS

2. The resulting score represents the relative priority of each backlog item.

Step 4. Order the Priorities:

1. Sort the backlog items in descending order based on their WSJF scores.

2. Items with higher WSJF scores should be prioritized and addressed first, as they are perceived to provide the highest value and carry the most significant cost of delay.

Step 5. Validate and Refine:

1. Review the prioritized backlog with the team, stakeholders, and any relevant parties.

2. Validate the WSJF scores and the resulting prioritization by considering feedback, additional insights, and constraints.

3. Refine the scores and priorities, if necessary, based on further discussions and analysis.

Step 6. Continuously Review and Adapt:

1. Backlog prioritization is an iterative process, and it should be revisited regularly.

2. Continuously review and update the WSJF scores and priorities based on changing business needs, market dynamics, business feedback, and project goals.

Consider Dynamic Value Curation as an alternative to WSJF. This approach eliminates subjective scoring, leveraging all available data to objectively compare the Net Present Value and cost of delay across competing initiatives.

Kano

The Kano Model helps categorize backlog items based on their impact on business satisfaction and their ability to meet business expectations. It considers the features or attributes that delight users, as well as those that are considered basic or essential.

Step 1. Identify Business Needs:

1. Conduct business research, surveys, interviews, or feedback analysis to identify and understand business needs, desires, and expectations related to the product or service.

2. Categorize the identified needs into different attribute types based on the Kano Model: Basic, Performance, Excitement, Indifferent, and Reverse.

Step 2. Categorize Backlog Items:

1. Map each backlog item to the appropriate attribute type in the Kano Model based on its potential impact on business satisfaction.

2. Basic Needs: These are fundamental user needs that businesses expect as a baseline. Not meeting these needs would result in significant dissatisfaction.

3. Performance Needs: These are features or improvements that directly impact business satisfaction. Meeting or exceeding these needs can positively influence business perception.

4. Excitement Needs: These are unexpected or innovative features that go beyond business expectations, providing delight and generating positive emotional responses.

5. Indifferent Needs: These are features that don't significantly impact business satisfaction. They can be low priority or considered optional.

6. Reverse Needs: These are features that, if present, decrease business satisfaction. They should be avoided or reevaluated.

Step 3. Prioritize Based on Attribute Importance:

1. Prioritize backlog items within each attribute category based on their importance and potential impact on business satisfaction.

2. Consider factors such as business feedback, market trends, business goals, and the competitive landscape when determining the priority within each category.

3. Focus on addressing basic needs first to ensure a solid foundation of business satisfaction, then move on to performance needs and excitement needs.

Step 4. Validate and Refine:

1. Share the prioritized backlog with stakeholders and the development team to gather feedback and ensure alignment.

2. Validate the categorization of backlog items and refine the priorities based on additional insights, discussions, and analysis.

3. Continuously reassess and update the backlog prioritization as new information or business feedback becomes available.

Feature-Gap Analysis

Checklist Comparison

Steps:

1. Identify products offered by leading competitors that are relevant to your software.

2. Create a Feature List: Start by listing all the features for both pieces of software. This can be done by reviewing documentation, marketing materials, or through hands-on exploration.

3. Organize Features: Group similar features together under relevant categories (e.g., User Interface, Security, Reporting).

4. Side-by-Side Comparison: Place the features of both software in a table, with one column for each software. Mark which software has which features.

5. Identify Gaps: Highlight or note where one software has a feature the other does not, or where the functionality differs significantly.

Outcome: A clear visual representation of which software has more or fewer features, and where specific gaps exist.

SWOT Analysis

Steps:

1. List Strengths: Identify what each software does well. This could be a broad range of features, ease of use, or performance metrics.

2. List Weaknesses: Determine where each software falls short. This might include missing features, poor user experience, or lack of scalability.

3. Identify Opportunities: Consider how the software could be improved or expanded. What features could be added, or what markets could be better served?

4. Identify Threats: Look at external factors that could negatively impact the software's success, like emerging competitors or technology changes.

Outcome: A structured view of each software's strengths and weaknesses, and insights into potential areas for improvement or risks.

User Journey Mapping

Steps:

1. Identify Key User Personas: Determine who the primary users of the software are and what their goals are.

2. Map the User Journey: Break down the user's interaction with the software into stages (e.g., Onboarding, Daily Use, Problem Resolution).

3. Compare Experiences: For each stage, compare how both software options support the user. Identify any pain points or missing features that could hinder the user experience.

4. Document Gaps: Highlight stages where one software falls short or lacks features that are crucial to the user's journey.

Outcome: A detailed view of how well each software supports users throughout their journey, with gaps clearly identified.

Feature Mapping

Steps:

1. Create a Feature Map: Draw a diagram that shows all the major features of both software products. Use shapes or icons to represent different features and connect them with lines if they are related.

2. Categorize Features: Organize features into logical groups (e.g., Core Functions, Advanced Features, Integrations).

3. Visualize Gaps: Use different colours or symbols to indicate which features are present in one software but missing in the other.

4. Review and Analyze: Step back and look at the feature map to easily see where one software might be lacking or where there is overlap.

Outcome: A visual representation of both software's features, making it easy to spot missing functionalities or redundancies.

Benchmarking

Steps:

1. Define Benchmarks: Identify industry standards, best practices, or features offered by leading competitors that are relevant to your software.

2. Assess Each Software Product: Compare both pieces of software against these benchmarks. Note where each software meets, exceeds, or falls short of the benchmarks.

3. Document Gaps: Clearly document the areas where the software fails to meet the established benchmarks.

4. Provide Recommendations: Based on the gaps identified, suggest areas for improvement or highlight where one software has a competitive advantage.

Outcome: A comparison of both software products against industry benchmarks, helping to identify areas where each may need enhancement or where one has a strategic advantage.

Guidance on Types of Survey/Feedback Data

Both qualitative and quantitative data are valuable for understanding your business partners' needs. Qualitative data provides rich, in-depth insights into their experiences and perspectives, while quantitative data allows you to measure trends, identify patterns, and make data-driven decisions. By combining both types of data, you can gain a comprehensive understanding of your business partners' needs and align your product vision accordingly.

Qualitative Data

- Open-Ended Responses: Surveys and feedback forms can include open-ended questions that allow business partners to provide detailed, descriptive answers. This data can help you understand their pain points and objectives, and the specific challenges they face.

- Feedback and Suggestions: Business partners may provide suggestions for improvements, new features, or changes to existing functionalities. This qualitative feedback can help you uncover innovative ideas and address specific pain points that may not have been identified otherwise.

- User Stories and Narratives: Surveys and feedback forms can invite business partners to share their stories or narratives about their experiences with the product. These stories provide context and deeper insights into how the product is used, the impact it has, and any challenges they encounter.

- Descriptive Data: Apart from written responses, qualitative data can also include descriptive information such as job roles, department affiliations, or specific use cases. These details provide a broader understanding of the user's context and allow you to tailor your product strategy accordingly.

Quantitative Data

- Likert Scale Ratings: Surveys can include Likert scale questions where business partners rate various aspects of the product, such as usability, performance, or satisfaction. The responses can be analyzed statistically to measure average ratings and identify trends or areas of improvement.

- Multiple-Choice Questions: Surveys can include multiple-choice questions to gather quantitative data on specific features, preferences, or usage patterns. Analyzing these responses can provide insights into which features are most important or commonly used by business partners.

- Net Promoter Score (NPS): NPS is a widely used metric that measures the likelihood of business partners recommending your product to others. By asking a simple question like, "On a scale of 0–10, how likely are you to recommend our product to a colleague?" you can calculate the NPS and track changes over time.

- Demographic Information: Surveys and feedback forms can include demographic questions to collect quantitative data on factors such as age, gender, or department. This data can be useful for segmenting responses and identifying patterns or differences in needs based on different demographic groups.

- Usage Statistics: In addition to surveys, you can also collect quantitative data directly from the product itself. By tracking usage metrics, such as the frequency of feature usage or time spent on different tasks, you can gain insights into how business partners interact with the product and identify areas for improvement.

Defining Clear Objectives

During many activities (e.g., meetings, interviews, usability testing, developing software), defining clear objectives is the first step. This means setting specific and measurable goals that guide the purpose and outcomes of these activities. It helps ensure that everyone involved has a shared understanding of what needs to be accomplished and provides a focus for the discussions or evaluations. When creating objectives for these types of activities, consider the following aspects:

Purpose and Scope

- Clearly articulate the purpose of the meeting, interview, or usability testing. Identify the specific area, topic, or goal you want to address.

- Define the scope or boundaries of the discussion or evaluation to ensure that it stays focused and relevant.

Desired Outcomes

- Identify the desired outcomes or deliverables that you expect from the activity. What do you hope to achieve or gain from the meeting, interview, or usability testing?

- Ensure that the outcomes are actionable and provide meaningful insights or progress toward a specific goal.

Specificity and Measurability

- Make the objectives specific and measurable, using clear language and concrete terms.

- Define what success looks like for each objective so that it can be evaluated or assessed.

User-Centric Considerations

- Keep the user or stakeholder perspective in mind when creating objectives. What insights, feedback, or information are you seeking from users or participants?

- Ensure that the objectives align with user needs, pain points, preferences, or expectations.

Relevance and Prioritization

- Prioritize the objectives based on their importance and relevance to the overall goal or project.
- Focus on objectives that have the most significant impact on decision-making, product improvements, or meeting outcomes.

Feasibility and Resources

- Consider the feasibility of achieving the objectives within the available resources, time, and constraints.
- Ensure that the objectives are attainable and realistic given the context and resources at hand.

Communication and Alignment:

- Clearly communicate the objectives to all participants or stakeholders involved, ensuring that they understand the purpose and desired outcomes.
- Seek alignment and agreement from relevant parties to ensure that everyone is working toward the same objectives.

Objectives and Key Results (OKRs) and Key Performance Indicators (KPIs)

This appendix is here to provide additional guidance for how to use OKRs or KPIs for internal software. Success occurs when you meet your goals, and you can't meet goals that are not clearly defined.

OKRs

OKRs (Objectives and Key Results) are a goal-setting framework that helps organizations define and measure their objectives. While OKRs should be specific to your product, the following are some generic measures that may help you formulate OKRs.

Objective 1: Enhance Efficiency in Investment Processes

Key Result 1: Reduce the average turnaround time for investment approvals by X% through process automation and optimization within the next six months.

Key Result 2: Achieve X% reduction in manual effort and administrative tasks related to investment management by implementing streamlined workflows and integrations.

Key Result 3: Implement X new features or enhancements to the product that improve efficiency and productivity in investment processes.

Objective 2: Ensure Data Accuracy and Integrity

Key Result 1: Improve data accuracy by reducing data-entry errors and inconsistencies by X% within the next quarter.

Key Result 2: Establish data-quality standards and achieve a data-quality score of X (measured by data integrity, completeness, and compliance) by the end of the year.

Key Result 3: Conduct regular data audits and resolve X% of identified data-quality issues within defined timeframes.

Objective 3: Enhance User Satisfaction and Experience

Key Result 1: Increase overall user satisfaction ratings (measured by surveys or feedback) to X on a scale of 1–10 within the next six months.

Key Result 2: Achieve an NPS (Net Promoter Score) of X by the end of the year, indicating a high level of user advocacy and recommendation.

Key Result 3: Implement X user-requested features or enhancements based on user feedback to enhance the user experience.

Objective 4: Foster Continuous Improvement and Innovation

Key Result 1: Conduct X number of retrospective sessions to gather insights and identify opportunities for process improvement and innovation.

Key Result 2: Implement X improvements or innovations based on the outcomes of the retrospective sessions within defined timeframes.

Key Result 3: Foster a culture of experimentation and learning by encouraging X% of team members to participate in innovation initiatives or learning activities.

These sample OKRs provide a framework for measuring the performance of a product that supports the investment lifecycle internally. However, it's important to customize the OKRs to align with the business's specific goals, priorities, and desired outcomes. Regular review, tracking, and adjustment of OKRs will help ensure ongoing progress and improvement.

KPIs

KPI stands for Key Performance Indicator. KPIs are used to monitor performance, identify areas of improvement, and track the success or effectiveness of various processes, projects, or initiatives within an organization.

KPIs serve as quantifiable indicators that provide insights into the performance and health of different aspects of an organization. They are often tied to specific objectives and are used to measure progress, compare against targets, and make data-driven decisions.

The following are examples of KPIs that may be relevant to your product.

User Satisfaction:

- Conduct periodic surveys or gather feedback to measure user satisfaction.

- Assess user satisfaction through ratings, Net Promoter Score (NPS), actual usage of the feature, or other qualitative and quantitative measures.

- This KPI reflects the perceived value, usability, and overall user experience of the product.

Time to ROI:

- Measure the time it takes for the organization to achieve a return on investment (ROI) from the product / new feature.

- Track the duration from the initial implementation or launch to when the product delivers measurable benefits or cost savings.

- This KPI indicates the efficiency and effectiveness of the product in supporting the investment lifecycle.

Cost Savings or Efficiency Gains:

- Quantify the cost savings or efficiency gains achieved using the product.

- Measure reductions in manual effort, time saved, or financial savings resulting from improved processes or automation.

- This KPI demonstrates the impact of the product in optimizing the investment lifecycle.

Cycle Time or Turnaround Time:

- Track the time it takes for specific tasks or processes within the investment lifecycle to be completed using the product.

- Measure the cycle time or turnaround time from initiation to completion.

- This KPI indicates the efficiency and speed of the product in facilitating investment-related activities.

Data Accuracy or Quality:

- Assess the accuracy, completeness, and quality of data managed by the product.

- Measure data-quality metrics, such as data integrity, error rates, or compliance with data standards.

- This KPI ensures the reliability and integrity of the data used in the investment lifecycle.

These KPIs provide a starting point for measuring the performance and impact of a product that supports the investment lifecycle within an organization. It's important to tailor the KPIs to the specific goals, objectives, and context of the organization and regularly review and update them to ensure their relevance and effectiveness.

Practical Applications of LAP in the Product-Management Lifecycle

Ideation and Market Research Phases: LAP encourages Product Managers to conduct thorough market research and ideation sessions utilizing agile methodologies. This ensures a comprehensive understanding of available Vendor-SaaS solutions against the backdrop of the organization's unique needs. Engaginjg cross-functional teams during these phases ensures diverse insights, leading to a more informed decision-making process.

Strategy and Roadmap Development: Applying LAP during the strategy development phase involves mapping out a flexible yet detailed path for software implementation, whether it involves a vendor or internal development. LAP's iterative nature allows Product Managers to adjust this roadmap as new information and technologies emerge, ensuring the software solution remains aligned with long-term strategic goals.

Definition and Design Coordination: In scenarios involving vendors, LAP principles guide Product Managers in effectively collaborating with vendors to tailor SaaS products to the organization's needs. This might include customizing user interfaces, integration with existing databases, or specific security enhancements, all negotiated and managed under LAP frameworks to ensure timely and effective delivery.

Implementation and Launch: LAP supports a structured yet flexible implementation strategy, ensuring that whether deploying a vendor's solution or rolling out an internally developed application, the process is smooth and adaptable to feedback. This includes efficiently managing timelines, resource allocation, and stakeholder expectations.

Performance Metrics and Analysis: Finally, LAP aids in establishing clear metrics and performance indicators crucial for evaluating the success of the implemented solution. Whether tracking the customization capabilities of an internally built application or assessing the impact of a Vendor-SaaS solution on operational efficiency, LAP provides the frameworks for continuous evaluation and improvement.

Competency Model

This model illustrates the types of skills that support product management.

Competency	Description	Basic	Intermediate	Advanced
Stakeholder Management	Engage and manage relationships with stakeholders to align product goals.	Identifies key stakeholders, engages occasionally, relies on senior management for guidance.	Regularly communicates with stakeholders, manages expectations, resolves minor conflicts, seeks broader input.	Anticipates needs and conflicts, leads alignment sessions, manages complex relationships independently.
User Needs Gathering	Elicit, document, and prioritize user needs to meet organizational needs.	Participates in sessions, documents results, needs guidance on prioritization.	Leads sessions, prioritizes needs, translates user needs into actionable tasks, balances conflicting needs.	Innovates in gathering techniques, integrates cross-departmental needs, drives product vision.
Product Strategy & Roadmap	Define product vision, set goals, and create a roadmap aligned with business objectives.	Understands strategy components, contributes to the roadmap with guidance.	Develops and manages the roadmap, aligns it with goals, adapts based on feedback.	Shapes overall strategy, aligns with long-term objectives, innovates in roadmapping.
Data-Driven Decision-Making	Leverage data and metrics to inform decisions and measure success.	Understands basic metrics, uses data with guidance, limited in setting new metrics.	Uses data to inform decisions, sets KPIs, tracks progress, analyzes trends.	Masters analytics, integrates data into all aspects of management, innovates in metrics design.
Change Management	Manage and lead change initiatives, ensuring smooth transitions and adoption.	Understands change principles, follows predefined plans, requires support to handle resistance.	Leads initiatives, engages with teams, develops tailored strategies for resistance.	Designs complex strategies, handles high resistance, leads cultural-change initiatives.
Technical Literacy	Understand technical concepts to effectively manage product development.	Basic understanding of terminology, relies on technical teams for insights.	Solid understanding, engages in technical discussions, makes informed decisions.	Deeply understands technical landscape, influences decisions, bridges gaps between teams.

Competency	Description	Basic	Intermediate	Advanced
Communication Skills	Convey information clearly and effectively across the organization.	Communicates with immediate team, occasionally struggles with clarity or audience adaptation.	Communicates vision and goals effectively, adapts style to different audiences.	Master communicator, influences and persuades stakeholders at all levels, tailors complex messages effectively.
Innovation & Creativity	Think creatively and innovate within product management, pushing boundaries.	Applies standard practices, occasionally contributes new ideas.	Regularly generates creative solutions, incorporates innovation into the product lifecycle.	Champions a culture of innovation, leads brainstorming sessions, implements breakthrough solutions.
User Experience (UX) Design	Understand and apply UX principles to create user-friendly internal products.	Understands basic UX principles, works with designers, limited ability to evaluate UX.	Collaborates with UX teams, integrates principles into design, advocates for user-centric choices.	Leads UX strategy, critiques and improves design, ensures alignment with user needs and business goals.

References

Much of the material in this book is from general knowledge I have acquired over the years. Some of the sources are books, articles, and websites, as well as real-life experiences.

Books

Cagan, M. (2008). *Inspired: How to Create Products Customers Love*. O'Reilly Media.

Croll, A., & Yoskovitz, B. (2013). *Lean Analytics: Use Data to Build a Better Startup Faster*. O'Reilly Media.

Doerr, J. (2018). *Measure What Matters: How Google, Bono, and the Gates Foundation Rock the World with OKRs*. Penguin.

Eyal, N. (2014). *Hooked: How to Build Habit-Forming Products*. Penguin.

Kleiner, M. (2023). *Lean-Agile Procurement: How to Get Twice the Value in Half the Time*. Mirko Kleiner.

Knapp, J., Zeratsky, J., & Kowitz, B. (2016). *Sprint: How to Solve Big Problems and Test New Ideas in Just Five Days*. Simon & Schuster.

Patton, J., & Economy, P. (2014). *User Story Mapping: Discover the Whole Story, Build the Right Product*. O'Reilly Media.

Pereira, D. (2024). *Untrapping product teams: Simplify the complexity of creating digital products* (1st ed.). Addison-Wesley Professional.

Perri, M. (2018). *Escaping the Build Trap: How Effective Product Management Creates Real Value*. O'Reilly Media.

Pink, D. H. (2009). *Drive: The Surprising Truth About What Motivates Us*. Riverhead Books.

Ries, E. (2011). *The Lean Startup: How Today's Entrepreneurs Use Continuous Innovation to Create Radically Successful Businesses.* Crown Business.

Torres, T. (2021). *Continuous Discovery Habits: Discover Products that Create Customer Value and Business Value.* Product Talk Publishing.

Wodtke, C. (2016). *Radical Focus: Achieving Your Most Important Goals with Objectives and Key Results.* Boxes and Arrows.

Research Papers and Articles

Agile Business. (n.d.). *Chapter 10: MOSCOW Prioritisation.* https://www.agilebusiness.org/dsdm-project-framework/moscow-prioritisation.htm

Agile Practices in Product Management: the Framework for Innovation. (2020). The Product Coalition Blog. https://productcoalition.com/agile-practices-in-product-management-the-framework-for-innovation

Clark, H. (2024, October 22). *What is value vs effort matrix and how does it work in product management?* theproductmanager.com. https://theproductmanager.com/topics/value-vs-effort-matrix/

Colotla, I., Fookes, W., Iverson, T., Schaefer, E., Sellschop, R., & Wijpkema, J. (2024, January 19). *Today's good to great: Next-generation operational excellence.* McKinsey & Company. https://www.mckinsey.com/capabilities/people-and-organizational-performance/our-insights/todays-good-to-great-next-generation-operational-excellence

Koch, T., Strube, G., & Tan, K. T. (2013, February 1). *Unleashing long-term value through operations excellence.* McKinsey & Company. https://www.mckinsey.com/capabilities/operations/our-insights/unleashing-long-term-value-through-operations-excellence

Stein, D. (2021, October 13). *How companies can improve employee engagement right now.* Harvard Business Review. https://hbr.org/2021/10/how-companies-can-improve-employee-engagement-right-now

The role of product management in the modern enterprise. (2020). McKinsey & Company. https://www.mckinsey.com/business-functions/mckinsey-digital/our-insights/the-role-of-product-management-in-the-modern-enterprise

Understanding and managing different types of product requirements. (2021). Harvard Business Review. https://hbr.org/2021/02/understanding-and-managing-different-types-of-product-requirements

Websites and Blogs

Journey to VMO. (n.d.). https://www.actionlearningjourney.com/journey-to-vmo

Mind the Product. (2025, January 22). https://www.mindtheproduct.com/

Roman Pichler's product management blog. (2023, April 11). Roman Pichler. https://www.romanpichler.com/blog

Stansell, J. (n.d.). *Product Coalition | Jay Stansell | Substack*. https://productcoalition.com/

Toxboe, A. (2023, February 10). *Buy a Feature*. Learning Loop. https://learningloop.io/glossary/buy-a-feature

Verduyn, D. (2020, November 11). *Home*. Kano Model. https://kanomodel.com/

www.ingramcontent.com/pod-product-compliance
Lightning Source LLC
Chambersburg PA
CBHW080424060326
40689CB00019B/4364